Jacques Leclerc

THIS DAY I

Preface by Roger Garaudy

Translated by Dinah Livingstone

ORBIS BOOKS

Maryknoll, New York 10545

The Catholic Foreign Mission Society of America (Maryknoll) recruits and trains people for overseas missionary service. Through Orbis Books Maryknoll aims to foster the international dialogue that is essential to mission. The books published, however, reflect the opinions of their authors and are not meant to represent the official position of the society.

First published in French as *Le Jour de l'Homme* by Editions du Seuil, Paris, © Editions du Seuil 1976

Translation © The Society for Promoting Christian Knowledge and Orbis Books 1980

U.S. edition 1980 by Orbis Books, Maryknoll, N.Y. 10545

Library of Congress Card Number: 80-50314
ISBN: 0-88344-504-2

Printed and bound in Great Britain

*Tant que j'aurai
mon cœur et ma folie . . .*
ARAGON

Contents

Acknowledgements

Thanks are due to Editions du Seuil for permission to include 'Hosties Noires' by L. S. Senghor in *Le Jour de l'Homme* by Jacques Leclercq, 1976.

Extracts from the Jerusalem Bible, published and © 1966, 1967, and 1968 by Darton, Longman & Todd Ltd and Doubleday and Co. Inc., are used by permission of the publishers. All other biblical quotations are from the Revised Standard Version of the Bible, copyrighted 1946, 1952, © 1971, 1973 by the Division of Christian Education of the National Council of the Churches of Christ in the U.S.A., are used by permission.

Preface

I like this long cry of joy of a liberated man. This hope hormone. I find in the book the same human warmth, the same vitality that one experiences in personal contact with its author Jacques Leclercq, that blaze of life, when he brings alive for us his love of Africa, his twelve years in Cameroon, among the Ewondo, or when his sermons grip us in Notre-Dame.

These pages are the living of a presence and a love, the witness of a life lit up by that love and that presence of the living Christ, the human Christ.

The evangelists' main concern was to show that Christ was God. Jacques Leclercq testifies with passion that this God is a man.

Jacques Leclerq has helped me at such a deep level in my own journey because it became clearer and clearer to me that there was no break between his passionate love for the God-man and the most passionate love of mankind.

The marvel is that he talks about Christ in such a human language, not as a philosopher nor even as a theologian, but as a witness. He recreates, like a poet, the experience of this primary human dimension, faith lived with joy in a life of love and hope.

At the other extreme from a negative theology which tells us all that God isn't, Jacques Leclercq exclaims to us, 'See what human joy and freedom are when you are in Christ and Christ is in you.'

It is true that the primary experience is that of negation. Millions of men and women for whom so much has been killed by the routine of every day can experience this at first only as an absence, a void to be filled.

Faith, this way of living with the life of all, of being responsible for the future of all, of realizing that our history hasn't already been written, isn't over, but has to be invented, invented by all, this faith must take root in today's problems, in the most painful, most immediate, most humdrum problems.

How can we get away from elementary anguish, protest,

and revolt to be able to discern the deeper movement which provokes them, their meaning and direction?

How can the need for faith show itself today in the ordinary experience of the life of the multitudes and how is that need to be met?

Faith cannot any longer take root in fear, in the feeling of helplessness before the forces of nature, as it did in pre-technological societies.

Human beings start with the conviction that they are the rulers of nature, and when this mastery fails they question the need and the value of this rule.

Faith can no longer take root in fear of power in society or respect for it. Even if the machinery of it is a puzzle for them, people no longer regard it as something mysterious; they may fear it, but they despise it and keep trying to escape from it.

In our time faith grows out of a feeling of mutilation. Alienated, repetitive work, the false positivist religion of technology and management, the scientism which claims to reduce everything to reason and cannot give human beings goals, all this today engenders questioning and revolts inspired by the confused sense of having had a primary and fundamental dimension amputated, the specifically human dimension of creation.

The enemy of all faith is always self-satisfaction and complacency. The problem is to bring home to people who are dissatisfied, who challenge the existing order, who rebel, that their effort to break the circle of being is the sign of a deeper desire, that they are indwelt by other people and indwelt by God.

The problem is to help them to make the primary demand, in the face of a world all of whose structures tend to stifle it, the demand for their inheritance as children of God.

The primary mediator is perhaps the poet. The poet breaks with the dehumanizing positivism which tries to convince us that everything which cannot be reduced to abstract reason does not exist and imprisons us in a world of immutable things, in the circle of being.

Beyond the concept, which manipulates objects, there is love which calls to subjects, there are utopia and poetry, which indicate projects and arouse in us a desire to carry them out.

That is what the marchers of 1968 spontaneously felt when they flung in the face of the old rigid world the explosive challenge, 'All power is imagination!'

We must restore to poetic language its ontological signifi-
cance as a pointer to transcendence, as a proclamation and
leaven of the future, as the creator of being, of the new way of
being.

Poetry, and art in general, is not just a language: it reminds
human beings that the possible is part of the real, that the real
is not just what already exists, the so-called circle of being. It
reminds us that the most real reality is created by our freedom.

God is not of the same order as words and things. He belongs to the order of poetry. He can only be talked about in
images. In the images of every period and every people. In
images which make us feel that there is no circle of being, but
that there exists an infinity of possibilities, that I can never
conceive of or imagine more than a fraction of reality.

To express faith in the language of our time means to help
people to realize that creation is not finished. That the act of
God is to create. That God is act, the act of love, the act of
liberation.

What strikes me first of all and seems to me essential in this
day of man, in this day of man's creation, is that its faith is first
of all an appeal to freedom.

The Bible, the gospel, a school of freedom! Faith, the practice of that freedom.

Faith, creative action to break the circle of being. To rescue
us from the influences which determine our lives, from everything which would make our lives the mere sum or product of
what our individual histories have made us, our families, our
cultures, our classes, our epoch.

Faith is act. An act is the opposite of entropy, of that drift
towards death which seems to be the law of things destined to
suffer an irreversible decline of energy and a decomposition of
structures. The act, and above all the act of faith, the specifically human act, the one preceded by an awareness of its project and directed by that project, is a challenge to entropy, an
ascent towards the improbable . . . Forgive me. I'm starting to
say in too abstract terms what this powerful book of Jacques
Leclercq's says to us in a hymn which takes us much further
out of ourselves.

The foundation of this freedom is the hope of the resurrection. 'Man,' he writes, 'has had hope planted in him.' The

resurrection is, *par excellence*, this challenge to entropy, to the forces of death, to all the powers which destroy human beings. A challenge to entropy, a wager against entropy. Such is the act which makes us human.

'Man *is* relation to God,' writes Jacques Leclercq. That God is a God who cannot be captured by our eyes, by our hands, by our minds, but can be by this act, this faith, this act of faith, this challenge, this wager. This challenge and this wager which set us on our feet, which set us moving to perform our human task. God is the specifically human dimension.

This freedom is the opposite of individualism. First of all it is love. Love is another name for faith. Before it is a feeling, love, like faith, is a way of being; like faith, it is what calls us out of ourselves. Freedom is the opposite of individualism. It is going out of ourselves towards a being who is greater than our individual selves, the one I see in another person's look, the one I hear in another's cry, the one who rescues me from my sensitive individualism to make me live the only experience which is worth living to the end. This experience is the realization that I only exist when I am indwelt by others, that I only exist as a participant in the total project of making man, each and every man, a man; in other words, a creator of his own life and his history. The incarnation has taught us that man's divine vocation is 'to move from just being oneself to creating oneself'.

'The word salvation means liberation,' writes Jacques Leclercq, joining the great Latin American current of 'liberation theology'. 'The gospel,' he adds, 'is general mobilization; it forces us to fight on all fronts.' Including the political front, which isn't just about how to get power, but is firstly thinking about the ends of society and the struggle to realize all human possibilities, the transformation of the world, participation in the completion of creation. We are still prehistoric men, wrote Marx: our history is barely separate from biological evolution, which is made up of competition, collisions and destruction. There is still a long way to go before we enter a really human history, made by all and not by some, made up of creations – it is the beginning of the poem of the universe. And the poem is meant to become a love poem.

This road goes through the liberation struggles of the

peoples of the Third World, through the revolutionary struggles of all.

Nor is this liberation partial. It develops on all levels 'on all fronts', as Leclercq writes: national liberation, social liberation, political liberation, and also (since it is not possible to transform the world without transforming oneself or to envisage genuine socialism without questioning a model of growth based on the blind and selfish manipulation of desire) liberation from sin, that is from egoistic turning-in on oneself, liberation from death, liberation from the law. 'Freedom is a permanent creation.'

In this way Father Leclercq gives full meaning to the words from the Epistle to the Galatians which he is fond of quoting, 'Brothers, you were called to freedom' (5.13).

ROGER GARAUDY

Introduction

There comes a day when you know you must write. Here I am with a blank sheet of paper in front of me and my mind teeming with thoughts about God, man, the couple, the world, life, and the mystery of the person: tenderness, intelligence, freedom.

I must write and try to say things there was no time for in a short interview.

About all those faces.

All those faces fraught with anguish, ravaged by distress, so many broken loves. Faces whose expressions were hungry with hope and which shattered me.

I must write about despair: it is always wrong. About humiliation, disappointment, and failure, which on closer examination always turn out to be a cry for tenderness. I must write about and face the absurdity of death. I must try to disclose the face of Jesus Christ, in which I wanted to lose myself and for which I have given my whole life. In his expression anguish, pain, and desolation are strangely akin to serenity, gentleness, and freedom. I want to show his face in which all the world's pain and God's tenderness are mingled.

I must write to be faithful to humanity, and say that there are no damned, that no single case is desperate, and that the world is groping forward, unsteadily perhaps, but forward towards success. Countless men and women have come to me at Notre-Dame in Paris, not because it was me but because this famous cathedral has been a place to come to and confess and seek reconciliation, for the last 800 years. They came to tell their grief, their rebellion, or to whisper the secret humiliation gnawing at their hearts like a cancer. Suffering had made their faces vulnerable as children's but they found peace and were often transformed before my eyes, not by the words I said, but because their confession released the best in themselves which was often hidden deep down but suddenly welled up through all the heavy oppressive layers which covered it. At last they felt it was possible to live freely and to love, to be themselves, eager to grow and capable of dreaming.

The whole of humanity is in every human being, in all human beings. This truth has been indelibly impressed on me by all my experience.

I do not write for those who share my faith. I do not write for unbelievers. I refuse to separate those who believe from those who do not.

There is tenderness: it is the same achievement.

There is intelligence: it is the same light.

There is freedom: it is the same passion.

There is death: it is the same terror. It requires great courage to live facing future annihilation. It also requires great courage to 'believe' in resurrection.

And the face of Jesus. God became man. This means that humanity is something fine. This is my faith. This is my destiny, my freedom, and my love.

Faith is personal. I do not 'have' my faith. I 'am' my faith.

But I do not feel different or alien from unbelievers. I feel fraternal. Not the devout and patronizing brotherhood which seeks to 'convert' unbelievers, but the human brotherhood in which faith and unbelief speak to each other, sharing the same pain and the same hopes. We have already come far when we ask the same questions about human destiny. I would even be prepared to say that it doesn't matter that we find different answers: we have become one by asking the same questions. I do not want to live my faith in opposition to unbelief, but side by side. For is anyone a total unbeliever? Or anyone really a total believer? I have met unbelievers who were ablaze with light which warmed my heart. And I know very well that faith is also sometimes a dark night, through which we must proceed like rowers with our backs to the shore.

Francis Jeanson writes: 'I believe we must only believe in what we bet will happen.'[1]

My bet is the resurrection. (On condition that we rid the term 'bet' once and for all of the meaning given it by Pascal in relation to the objects of faith.) Demolish the whole of theology with its dogmas, principles, and theses: this would not affect my faith in the slightest. Having faith means believing in someone. It is a living relationship. Faith is tenderness, sometimes even madness.

Faith and unbelief recognize their common need. This means they can try to come together and work out something beyond ideologies. They can try to create 'spaces of freedom' in the most demanding depths of our awareness, to make sense of our humanity.

At this level neither a passion for humanity nor a passion for God can be an alibi or a refuge: we must answer. Life itself sets the questions.

Then faith and unbelief can truly converse, not to hold forth, argue, convert, still less to come into conflict, but to share: freedom involves admiration and respect. We put ourselves at risk because we are together in truth. . . .

NOTE

1   *La Foi d'un incroyant*, p. 182.

Human Dimensions

Imagine a number of men in chains, all condemned to death and every day some are butchered in sight of the others. Those who remain see their own condition in that of their fellows; they look at each other painfully and without hope as they await their turn. This is the image of the human condition.
(Pascal, *Pensées*)[1]

We know the truth not only by reason but also with our hearts. It is in this latter way that we know the first principles, and reasoning, which has nothing to do with it, protests in vain.
(Pascal, *Pensées*)[2]

I have not learnt what I write from books. The first thing books have taught me is to beware abstraction: it is often the refuge of those who can offer nothing in their own lives in accordance with things that actually happen, and these happenings are not at all abstract but obstinately real. I have caught great minds *flagrante delicto* of dishonest abstraction. Life, public opinion, the movement of history, the political scene betrayed their ideas. So they took refuge in 'abstraction', to create a harmony within the scope of their principles, that they could not find in real events. But to refuse to countenance events because they will not submit to our abstractions is an opting out which shows complete. contempt for life.

I want to seek the universal in the depths of the inviolable solitude where I am most myself – a man. That is where it is rooted and that is where it creates its secret language which is beyond words, which makes communication possible with the fathomless mystery of the 'other', giving insight into his very soul.

I do not intend to argue about God but to tell plainly what my life – life – has taught me about humanity and its mystery. But I must confess that every time I have contemplated humanity, in myself or in others, I have always become aware of God as a sovereign presence. If I seek humanity at all its levels – courage, cowardice, pain, or joy – in the deepest depths of the human condition I always find its noblest dimension: God. But which God?

André Malraux was an agnostic. When faced with transcendence and haunted by death he said: 'St John writes, "God is love"; these words are the pivot on which all history has rocked.' These are the same three words which summon to judgement our definition both of God and of man.

It is the first time anyone dared 'define' God as love. Love is no longer only an attribute or quality of God (the Bible had already suggested that); it is his 'being', his life, his person.

Until then, human beings aware of their limitations and afraid of death, felt themselves controlled by terrifying gods, and the worn statues of ancient gods show us impassive faces with inscrutable expressions, whose only answer to questions of our destiny is to inspire fear.

And we know very well that if the gods of Sumeria, Assyria, Athens, and Rome reigned in darkness, today too, other gods as cruel, compelling, and tyrannical have taken their place: money, sex, power in all its forms.

These modern gods also have no face and no answer except hatred, fear, and derisive laughter. They enslave their followers, demand everything they have got, to the last shred of love, the last ounce of freedom.

We can only define a man by his god, because this god determines what are the real questions to ask or stifle.

A man may completely deafen the voice of conscience by constant business, work, pleasure, or passion. But a moment comes when he feels sick of the futile and inane and asks where he is really going. In this precious silence every man stands before his god whom he looks to for an answer.

If his god is money, sex, or power, his only answer will be despair which he must quickly stifle in another whirl of evasions.

If he himself is his own god, again his only answer will be anxiety, because in these special moments of clarity a man sees himself in all his limitations: he knows he cannot be self-sufficient. Once again he must escape from this implacable looking-glass which shows him what he looks like and thus reveals his god as dumb and derisory.

'God is love.' St John reveals a God who loves. And everything is turned upside down. History acquires eternal meaning. Love and freedom cannot die any more.

Tell me who is your god and I will tell you who you are.

This is where it becomes necessary to define man, because if he happens to meet this God on his way, he suddenly discovers the whole answer. He knows why he is alive. He knows why he has suffered, struggled and created.

He knows why he loves.

The sun and the flowers speak another language.

And music is eternal.

He knows what he is fighting for. Justice and peace are no longer mere words: they are a vocation.

He knows that the fleeting joys of his life, laughing and dancing and bodies embracing, are not provisional: they are a promise of fulfilment.

'God is love.' Agape: tenderness.

Meeting this God means you can hold a loved face between your hands and say the craziest words of love: 'I love you, so you will live.' And he who has come to the end of the road, when death knocks at his door and as the Bible says:

> . . . before the silver cord is snapped,
> or the golden bowl is broken,
> or the pitcher is broken at the fountain,
> or the wheel broken at the cistern. . . .   (Eccles. 12.6)

he whose turn has come to say the terrible words: 'I am going to die,' can defy death because he has the answer: he is a son of God and Jesus has arisen from the dead.

'God is love' – these three words to which all those who have faith have committed their lives, their power of loving, their freedom, their intelligence, these three words come from the First Epistle of the apostle John.

Perhaps this text should have priority for all those who are seeking how to apply the gospel in their lives, all who insist on being 'true to themselves', the essential criterion for which is perhaps the tension in trying to reconcile the ideal with experience, the generosity of efforts with their disappointing results, the thirst for the absolute with the evidence of our limitations, prayer with action, all those torn by the contradiction between death awaiting us somewhere in our own lives, death unpredictable but familiar, and resurrection which is perhaps possible but a complete unknown.

We should read and reread the First Epistle of John. It was written at the end of the first century. The Gospels were already familiar, the first heresies had arisen, gnosis in particular – a religion of knowledge, and John responds. In this epistle he appears as the last living apostle, the only one who can speak of Jesus as a friend speaks of a friend. He is wrapped up in long cogitated memories, ripened by experience, and his letter's grave serenity conveys his luminous awareness when he speaks of Jesus:

> which we have heard,
> which we have seen with our eyes,
> which we have looked upon
> and touched with our hands . . .
> we proclaim also to you. . . . (1 John 1–3)

Faith has no other support than this witness.

Of course, over the centuries, the Bible itself has drawn people to the contemplation of God. Great mystics like Abraham, Moses, and the prophets had learnt to see God's presence in history and there was a slow transition from the idea of a warrior god to the progressive revelation of a God who watches over us, loves and forgives us.

Of course there was the 'law', the charter of the covenant between God and his people, and Deuteronomy, six centuries before Christ, is the book closest to the Gospels. 'Thou shalt love thy God with all thy heart.'

And with the final books of the Old Testament the idea of the chosen people was expanded to include all mankind.

But this long history of a people groping towards its God is all leading up to the final revelation in which the God of Abraham, Isaac, and Jacob is offered to mankind in the person of Jesus, Son of God made man.

Then the old covenant becomes the 'new and everlasting' covenant. The ancient law becomes the new commandment: 'Love one another. . . .'

It is John, the disciple whom Jesus loved, who reveals to us not only the person of Jesus and its mystery but also the experience, that we can all share, of God's tenderness. And perhaps it is in this First Epistle of John that mankind is given a total definition and mankind's history its full meaning.

God is love, God is tenderness,
God is light.
It is not that we first loved God but that he first loved us.
God is love: he who abides in love abides in God.

We should read John's letter and be rocked by its calm
rhythm in which his thought proceeds with the tranquil solemnity of a Bach chorale. The language is simple but we recognize the balanced counterpoint of parallelisms so common
in Hebrew. It is more than a letter, it is a poem: its music is
expressive and its very silences reveal to us both God's tenderness and the beauty of humanity:

Beloved, let us love one another;
for love is of God. . . .
Beloved, if God so loved us,
we also ought to love one another.   (1 John 4.7, 11)

This is what God is. This is what man is.

John's First Epistle invites us to love not as good will, not
even as a duty, but as the expression of what we are. Not to
love is to lie.

If anyone says 'I love God' and does not love his brother, he
is a liar.

The only way to be true to ourselves and come into communion with God is to be capable of loving.

God is light. He who loves his brother dwells in the light.

Because love is in God. Love is of God.

Love is God and every human being is a son of God.

Henceforth all our most generous impulses, and the wonderful gift that each of us bears within him, love between men and
women, the delight of fiancés, the mother looking at her child,
honest friendship, shared bread, forgiveness offered and
accepted, grief comforted, the kindly smile and all the beauty
we see, all music and every work of art, the harmony of nature,
the sun and the sea, birds and flowers, the path through the
woods, the wind and the rain, and St Vincent de Paul and St
Francis of Assisi and J. S. Bach, and indeed every human
heart, and everything that makes us worthy and proud of our
humanity, all commingled in God's tenderness, is love.

Then fear is overcome. The fear of God – a scandal, a
heresy, a lie!

There is no fear in love,
but perfect love casts out fear.
For fear has to do with punishment,
and he who fears is not perfected in love.   (1 John 4.18)

Or:

In this is love perfected with us, that we may have confidence for the day of judgment. . . .   (1 John 4.17)

John makes 'God's judgement' which fills so many Christians with a cold fear and disgusts so many unbelievers, a reason for confidence and security. Because our God is a God who saves and his 'judgement' is 'reconciliation'. This is how he judges, like the great judges to whom the Bible dedicates a book because they are liberators of the people.

In this sense God is the sovereign judge and the 'Last Judgement' is God's final triumph over evil.

I am writing to you, little children, because your sins are forgiven. . . .   (1 John 2.12)

It is sufficient to love. Sufficient but also necessary.

By this we shall know that we are of the truth, and reassure our hearts before him. . . .   (1 John 3.19)

We must love, love truly, with a love that belongs to our very self, in which mind and feeling fuse, to give back the other to himself, help him create his own life and show him his own power of loving.

Little children, let us not love in word or speech but in deed and in truth.   (1 John 3.18)
But if any one has the world's goods and sees his brother in need, yet closes his heart against him, how does God's love abide in him?   (1 John 3.17)

At this level of charity all injustice is intolerable, all hatred and bitterness monstrous, and thus a Christian commits not only all he has but all he is to action, including political action, which thus attains its full dignity, and passes from words to deeds, from cry to challenge.

'We know that we are of God,' John proclaims, and this is the definition of humanity.

Loving God means believing in humanity, especially if it is

suffering or subject to evil. Despairing of a human situation
means denying God.

John's letter is the supreme Christian challenge to those who
cry out in despair against injustice, poverty, hatred, and war:
'We believe in love.'

No longer to believe in God because we are unable to reconcile people, the world, and life with what we thought we
knew about God, often means refusing to pass from 'belief' to
faith: at any rate it is a consecration of a caricature of God.

Do you refuse to admit an 'external' God, grand master of
the universe and ruthless lawgiver? A God up there? So do I.
Who could give his life for such a God? I have often found that
the God denied by many unbelievers is a God I do not believe
in either.

As long as we are only fighting against images, formulations,
concepts, dogmas, rites . . . can we really say: I do not believe
in God?

As long as we are only concerned with keeping laws, theological definitions, practices, texts petrified by untouchable traditions; in short, as long as we only have a belief, can we really
say: 'I believe in God'?

Belief believes in 'something'; it holds to dogmas, concepts,
notions, rites, principles, practices. It is often weighed down by
taboos and sometimes only sustained by fear. At its lowest level
it becomes superstition and magic.

Faith believes in 'someone'. This implies love and freedom. It
is not extra luggage added to our lives. It is not an acquisition,
not a result obtained once and for all: it is permanent tension.

It is not a simple intellectual adhesion to a set of dogmas,
not blind submission to a doctrine, however pure. Faith is not
a moral stance on a code or set of principles.

Faith is first and foremost the free attachment of my person
to the person of Jesus, God's revelation, and in order for this
relationship to be a true one it must be a relationship of love
and involve my whole life.

Faith is alive. It is a constant search and questioning. It is
an invitation to go ever further forward. It involves all our
capacity to love and is at the same time a call to freedom.

Then our hunger and thirst for the absolute, our insatiable
hunger for love, our thirst for freedom find their rightful
objects in Jesus the Son of God the Father who loves and saves

us, and this for each one of us is the realm of eternity.

He who comes to me will never hunger. He who believes in me will never thirst, says Jesus.

My faith carries me, with all my human limitations, into God's very self, as the river is carried, lost, and mingled with the ocean.

I am of God. This is the great cry of the apostle Paul.

I live, no not I, Christ lives in me.

Or again:

For me, to live is Christ.

Or in his very bold phrase:

We are of his race.

To be saved means knowing and living this. It is the experience of recreating in our own lives, in our own personal way, the experience to which the apostles bore witness: Jesus is risen.

This requires all our love.

Fiancés – affiance, confidence, fidelity, faith all have the same root – are two people who have 'faith' in one another. But they can only have this faith *because* they love. Their love becomes a living faith. In the twelfth century the words: 'I give you my faith' meant 'I love you'.

Thus the road of faith is inseparable from the gift of loving. I have no proofs, you will say, on which to base such a relationship with God? Well then! Would it still be faith if I had proof?

What sort of a love is it that demands proof? By dint of discussing the things of faith, reasoning, arguing, demonstrating, proving, we have reduced them to the level of 'problems'.

While God, Jesus, the gospel, the Church are studied as problems, faith does not come into it. The object of faith is not a problem, it is a mystery.

There is an order of problems and an order of mysteries. Just as in the Bible there is the level of the text and the level of the message the text conveys. There is the letter and the Spirit. And we have been warned: 'The letter kills.'

Our minds are made to tackle problems, analyse and solve them. They find pleasure in research and reasoning which leads to a solution. When the problem is solved, the question answered, the mind feels satisfied, happy, and fulfilled. Whether it is a problem of arithmetic or of walking on the moon, whether it requires a few minutes or millennia, the human mind knows that it has the power to solve, sooner or later, the problems set it by the universe.

Mystery also confronts the mind. But here the procedure is not the same and the way of knowing is different. It is no longer a matter of reasoning, or advancing step by step to a solution, but of plunging into its fullness as if it were the sea.

The mind becomes immersed in mystery. It sounds it but never reaches the bottom. The more it knows, the more it discovers, ever eager, ever satisfied.

This is contemplation. And it is the mind which contemplates. And when it returns, astounded, from the depths of the mystery, it can no longer speak of it with the arguments of the theologian and the philosopher: it needs all the resources of art and poetry. As did John of the Cross, Francis of Assisi, Teresa of Avila, Johann Sebastian Bach or Olivier Messiaen.

We cannot prove a mystery: we must bear witness to it. In faith – as in love – there are plenty of trials or proofs to test it under the harsh light of freedom and its requirements.

Indeed faith is often darkness, anguish, and dizziness. It is suffering. Belief can be a security. Faith is often insecurity. Then it gropes its way forward with only 'truth to itself' to guide it, and it uses the same language as wounded love when it is racked by doubt, and it masters its loneliness and grief in order to go on living. The faith, like love, becomes its own source of hope.

And the day comes when a moment of grace gives faith its fullness. Doubt is not resolved, it is dissolved, drowned. And then faith is no longer only attachment, acceptance, faithfulness: it is intuitive 'knowledge' of 'who God is'. It is contemplation. Faith becomes certainty. These great moments of awareness cannot be justified by reasoning. They cannot be explained in words any more than tenderness can be explained or justified.

'Illuminism', it will be said. No. I have met enough 'illuminati' in my life to be able to make this 'no' very firm. Illuminism is self-contemplation. It is fed by a febrile sensibility and cannot stand the test. Illuminism is a disease. Mysticism is a form of health. Illuminism is a complex, chattering, contemptible stupidity. Mystical contemplation is clear, sovereign, royal as the mind itself. Illuminati are irresponsible people crushed by the weight of their own egos. The great mystics carry great responsibility: they carry the world.

This is what I believe we should call the relationship of faith.

And it is not an exceptional situation: I have come across it in daily life at every cultural level, even the humblest, because this is one of the conditions of faith, the gentleness of humility to accept oneself as one is, complete with limitations, inadequacies, and unsatisfied dreams. To accept oneself 'as such'. Not wanting to be somebody else is the first step on the way to sanctity. I also believe it to be the first step on the way to freedom.

We were not taught this in the catechism, or in courses of religious instruction. So many young people reaching the age to take control of their lives, dazzled by their own strength, longing to 'be', claiming freedom, loving passionately, knowing now that they are 'somebody', a human person, are bitterly disappointed by the faith. They can offer the world and life opening before them nothing better to justify their faithfulness to God than the infantile vocabulary of their catechism, wretched constraints and fears, routines, taboos, rites, and practices alien and meaningless to their way of life.

When they come and tell me: 'I have lost the faith', I am not surprised but I ask for an explanation. Because what they are abandoning I threw out long ago. Often they have only lost their 'beliefs'. They 'return to themselves': the time for faith has come. They can no longer piously accept ready-made 'truths' or follow a road mapped out for them. They must create their own lives and compose in the depths of their awareness their own song of love and freedom. In these great bursts of energy we meet God.

The slightest hint of alienation in an act of faith betrays God and disfigures the person who makes it. God is liberation or he is not.

NOTES

1   Lafuma, 434.
2   Ibid., 110.

The Definition of Man: God
THE CREATION

Boldly the Bible begins: 'And God said: "Let us make man in our own image. . . ."'

The author of the first chapter of Genesis was a great poet, and also a great mystic. To define man he makes use of God, the source of his being and becoming. 'Let us make man in our own image. . . .'

This is just after he has portrayed for us the magnificent spectacle of the birth of the world. Darkness covered the abyss and only the Spirit brooded over the primal waters.

'Spirit' means breath, the very life of God the creator. The Spirit moved over the shapeless void and the life of the world began: for this moving of God's breath over the surface of the waters the Hebrew text uses a special word which means the flight of an eagle over its nest: thus, according to an ancient tradition, the eagle fertilized its eggs. It is significant that the Hebrew poet chose this word to describe the rush of God's living breath over the abyss. God is present, life is about to arise. The Bible God is the God of the living.

It is also significant that, centuries later, the gospel accounts of the baptism of Jesus transpose this scene with the Spirit, in the form of a dove passing over the waters of Jordan, for the 'new creation' this time and the gift of life that never dies.

This is not the place to give a detailed exegesis of the creation story. It is a marvellous text with a well-developed theology full of awe and wonder at nature, man, and God.

God said: 'Let there be light and there was light.' This light which came before the creation of all the luminaries – the sun, moon, and stars – was the bedazzlement of the great poet and mystic at the splendour of God and his creation: God is light.

And the six days of creation follow in an orderly manner with the rhythm and regular balancing of a Hebrew poem, with the constant refrain:

And God said . . . and God said . . .
And God saw that it was good.
And there was evening and there was morning. . . .

And then came the sixth day. Suddenly the tone changes. The rhythm is interrupted. It is as if God pauses for reflection before crowning his creation with his masterpiece.

'And God said: "Let us make man." ' He does not say: 'Let there be man', as in the formula for the preceding days which had created the light, set the stars in their places, and unfurled the seas. The plural of majesty impresses upon us the gravity of this moment when God himself – and the poet with him – marvels at this overflow of loving kindness in which he gives of himself to the uttermost.

> So God created man in his own image,
> in the image of God he created him;
> male and female he created them.   (Gen. 1.27)

It is important to translate the Hebrew as precisely as possible because the poet is telling us God's intention. Literally we should read:

> And God said: 'Let us make man' (*homo*: human being),
> in the image of God he created him;
> male (*vir*) and female (*mulier*) he created them.

'God is love' (1 John 4.16). That is the definition of him. He is in himself Gift, Welcome, and Exchange. We should think of the Trinity in the light of this truth: God's whole life is a triple outpouring of love, love so mutual that it is perfect unity, that ideal unity of which all lovers dream. And this love constantly flows outwards. When God created mankind he created it in the image of his own infinite tenderness, and the marvellous result was:

> And God created man in his own image,
> in the image of God he created him;
> male and female he created them.

This brings us to the great dignity of sexuality which celebrates tenderness. The man has the power of the gift and the woman the sweetness of welcome and the child they create is the visible sign of exchange.

Another Genesis poet – in chapter 2 – tells us an even simpler story of the creation of man and woman by God's hands.

This time God makes a clay statue with his hands: 'Then the LORD God formed man of dust from the ground' (Gen. 2.7).

The Hebrew word *adamah* meaning earth gives the man his name 'Adam'. Man is the 'earthy one'. This was a necessary attempt to explain every man's attachment to the earth, mother-earth, his earth, and his mysterious bond with the cosmos, the sun and the rain and the moon and the wind, and his mastery over the animal and vegetable kingdom. It was also a way of explaining death and the inexorable march towards old age which leads man back to the earth, the hole in the ground where he is covered and finally dissolved into dust. . . . The ancient text is telling us in a simple popular style, with simple images, the story which people told each other in the evenings in their tents at the time of the patriarchs: man is born of the earth.

This was a way of explaining man's nobility: his love, freedom, intelligence, conscience, goodness, creative power, and urge to develop. . . . Thus the ancient desert poet's deepest reflection on his life and destiny leads him to faith and his meditation on mankind leads him to God.

> Then the LORD God formed man of dust from the ground,
> and breathed into his nostrils the breath of life;
> and man became a living being.   (Gen. 2.7)

This is what often happens. I have met many people who discover God by discovering themselves in their most secret self-awareness, love, and freedom. Thus beyond all arguments and spiritual revolt, faith suddenly appears as 'being faithful to oneself'.

I discovered God in the definition of man by reading the Bible. But I did not believe just because I read it in the Bible. It was because I believed that I was able to 'read' it in the Bible.

> He breathed into his nostrils the breath of life;
> and man became a living being.

The breath of God, the Spirit, is the gift of life, and because in God loving is living, it is the gift of love. 'We are of God,' says John (1 John 4.6).

Some people might say that I am imagining things to escape from human reality, its limitations and the absurdity of death. But mystical life is a powerful force in man's most 'real' depths to satisfy his passion for the absolute in transcendence. Is transcendence imaginary? Then should we deny Mozart? I find 'what is greater than myself' within myself. It shakes my freedom and my power to love, thereby enhancing them. 'God exists, I have found myself.' God who is growth, God the creator.

This is probably the point at which the upward movement of my faith joyfully encounters the generous faith of my unbelieving friends, faith in mankind. We have often shared profound insights, and broken through ambiguity to privileged moments of communication where our beliefs met.

I like man as revealed by the ancient biblical text: formed of clay and breathed on by the divine. I like the Bible's purity – in both the New and the Old Testament – resolutely unaware of any dichotomy between body and soul. The thought of Plato and Descartes became petrified into an inhuman separation between the 'spiritual' soul and the 'carnal' body. A soul whose splendour was entombed in a body of sin. The Bible does not even have a Hebrew word for the body, except as a corpse. 'Flesh' in the Bible, including most of Paul's writings, is the human person, on its own without God; it is an admirable compound of the 'carnally spiritual' and 'spiritually carnal' as Péguy calls it. If you read all Paul's writings you will not find a single word about the 'immortal soul' and nothing is as irritating as the ridiculous language that talks about 'saving souls'. I want to save people.

And the Spirit, as we have seen, is God's breath. This is the struggle offered to my freedom between 'flesh and Spirit': to accept (or refuse) with my whole self, God's breath so that I 'become more' and continue the creation. This is a very different idea from that of an absurd struggle between body and soul and those sad moralities based on restrictions, negations, denials, and a despairing 'self-distrust'.

I'd like to contemplate gratefully the picture of a creator God breathing on a clay statue: it is a gesture of liberation. Man is sown with hope and his face is set towards the 'greater being' where he can fulfil his freedom.

As for the creation of woman, in the second Genesis account, although of course it bears the marks of a primitive mentality in which the man is the woman's lord and master, it tells us in a graphic way the biblical poet's thoughts on God's plan for the couple. 'It is not good for man to be alone,' says God. This

is an elementary reflection true of every man. . . . But what
interests me more, beyond the Hebrew author's naive expressions, is the expansion of 'looking at oneself' to find God looking at man.

Everyone knows the story of the creation of woman, man's
companion and 'helpmeet like himself' whom God forms from
Adam's side.

Of course woman had to come from man. How otherwise to
explain the male domination of women which has char-
acterized the human couple for millennia? And in particular
how otherwise to explain the perfect complementarity of the
couple, the heat of love and passion, the tension towards unity,
sexuality, and all forms of desire? This is already suggested in
the Hebrew vocabulary: *ish* (man) and *isha* (woman).

But the best thing in the story is the man's cry of wonder
when God brings the woman to him:

> This at last is bone of my bones and flesh of my flesh. . . .
>   (Gen. 2.23)

A cry of joy, especially when we remember that in Hebrew
'flesh' means 'person' and that among all the parts of the body
in which primitive peoples localized their feelings, the bone
was the deepest source of their self-awareness.

'Flesh of my flesh . . . bone of my bones.' It is the Hebrew
superlative like the 'holy of holies' or 'king of kings'. The first
man's great cry of happiness at the first woman is the cry of
every man – and we have all experienced it – when suddenly
love comes to him and he looks at her he loves.

'Truly this is flesh of my flesh, bone of my bones.' It is me,
my other self.

> God created man in his own image . . .
> male and female he created them.

This is the root of every human family. This is woman's
great vocation, to stimulate man so that he is revealed to himself. And man's great vocation is continually to know better
the face that opens before him and through him. Then the two
are completed in a trinity: their love becomes someone, for this
is the place of the child between his mother and father, he is
the third person in the unity of a single love.

Man and woman create new human beings. They are

united in their own happiness and their joy in their God, a God who is love. And every man and woman who love each other are a living flame for all eternity:

God created man in his own image . . .
male and female he created them.

Such is God. Such is man.

Yet, O LORD, thou art our Father;
we are the clay, and thou art our potter;
we are all the work of thy hand. (Isa. 64.8)

For millennia clay has been ennobled in man's hands to become a work of art. We should say repeatedly: even if the human condition too often reminds us of our earthy weight, and sometimes, despite ourselves, we are dragged down by our passions, man's nobility is the 'breath of God' which is the source of his joy, the only joy which transfigures the earth, the joy of loving and of being loved.

Having faith does not mean living in a state of humiliation, even less of resignation because we are but clay; it is living confidently in the potter's hands, and being able to recognize in events, even when they are contradictory, and in the harsh necessity to which we must submit each day, God's hands who made us 'in his image and likeness'.

Perhaps having faith means accepting that we are loved, loved by an optimistic God for whom all creation is a success, and to let things take their course as if we were surrendering into a loving Father's arms. I do not abdicate my freedom. I appeal to Jesus, to his final prayer which has become ours:

. . . all mine are thine,
and thine are mine. . . . (John 17.10)

What astonishing freedom and what boldness. Jesus has come to the end of his work, the end of his life and loyalty, and we find that this completely open relationship between Son and Father (which is the relationship between man and God), this total freedom of speech, are the fruit of total obedience, that admirable obedience where authority and acceptance are one with a common project: then obedience becomes creative because it is responsible, it is dynamic because it is a conversation, it is free because it is sharing.

31

Jesus offers us this boldness and freedom in our relationship with God – this is prayer. They come from a humble acceptance of what we are, in filial loyalty to God the Father who leads each one of us far beyond the limits of our freedom, the temporary setbacks of love, even beyond sin, towards our personal success, because since Jesus, we know that death itself is the perfect fulfilment of our whole life in resurrection, to the unutterable point in our story when the 'setting of man is the rising of God'.

In the same chapter of John when Jesus speaks to God about us, his prayer suddenly becomes anxious. He says:

I am praying . . . for those whom thou hast given me,
for they are thine;
. . . they are in the world. . . .   (John 17.9, 11)

Again we have the astonishing relationship between man and God: 'Father, they are thine. . . .' And our human condition in daily life: 'Father, they are in the world. . . .' In John's gospel the world is evil, chaos, revolt, refusal. They are in the world, they are in chaos, plagued by the furies of flesh and blood, delivered to evil, blinded by passions, beset by sin. . . . And then the conclusion like the sun coming out after the storm:

I am praying for them;
. . . they are mine.

Henceforth, whatever the level of faith, whatever the weight of sin, whatever setbacks or disappointments or misfortunes have befallen us, these words reach our innermost self to calm our anxiety and give us peace.

Having faith is to accept being loved. And with such a God, sin, the essential sin, is anxiety.

For my part I want to admit only one kind of anxiety: Jesus's anxiety when he speaks to his Father about us, the anxiety mingled with tenderness of bearing the burden of others, the poor, the oppressed, the hungry, people involved in war, people in despair. . . . 'Father, they are thine. I am praying for them. . . .'

The act of faith is saying 'yes' to this relationship of son to father, in which all love and freedom find their fulfilment, where life is defined as victory over death. . . .

What is love if we have to die? What is my freedom if there is no absolute? And what is absolute if there is no God?

History, technology, and politics which are a continual creation entrusted to our freedom, and everything on this earth which shows the love of man for man, can only find their 'meaning' and fulfilment in this filial relationship, this 'complicity' which connects us with God the Father.

This is Jesus's dream for the world:

Father, thou in me,
me in thee . . .
that they may be one.

The Covenant
DEFINING HISTORY: GOD

God said to Abram: 'Bring me a heifer three years old, a she-goat
three years old, a turtledove, and a young pigeon.'
And he brought him all these, cut them in two, and laid each half
over against the other; but he did not cut the birds in two.
And when birds of prey came down upon the carcasses, Abram drove
them away. . . .
When the sun had gone down and it was dark, behold, a smoking fire
pot and a flaming torch passed between these pieces.
On that day the LORD made a covenant with Abram, saying, 'To
your descendants I give this land. . . .'
(Gen. 15.9–11, 17–18)

Why are we quoting this strange story from the Book of Genesis? I want to investigate not only the literary beauty of the
poem but its source: the author's vision and inspiration, and
the point at which his meditation on man's destiny draws him
on to 'something greater than himself'. However, he does not
cease to be himself. He uses everyday words and describes rites
in use in his day: but he sees in history a mysterious current
running through all our meandering.

'Lift up your eyes and look,' said God.

When we discover the biblical poet at the point where he had
completely surrendered to transcendence, we receive today,
thousands of years later, the same revelation he had when he
told us the story of Abraham.

Apart from his prophetic vision, it is hard to see what this
ritual of blood and darkness and fire has to do with our
modern technological civilization.

However, what we have here is more than a piece of folk-
lore, and if this story told in the desert and as the flocks were
dozing, has come down through the millennia to our own
times, it is not just because it is a picturesque poetic tale of
mysterious ancient rites. It is because it has an essential message which I think concerns the whole of mankind and each
one of us.

34

The conversation between God and Abraham, which seems so naive to us, is the way in which ancient storytellers show us one of the patriarch's greatest mystical experiences and the relationship of friendship in which God wishes to be united with man.

The bloody scene set before us in which Abraham sacrifices a heifer, a goat, and a ram, cuts each animal in half and puts each half opposite the other, when amid the swooping birds of prey God comes with darkness as a smoking fire pot and flaming torch and passes between the pieces, is a contract ritual.

In fact this is how a contract was entered into in primitive times. Each party to the contract had to pass between the halves of the sacrificed animals and it was understood that anyone who broke the contract would undergo the fate of the slaughtered animals.[1]

Here it is God who enters into a contract. He contracts with man. The Bible, in telling us this unheard-of fact, could only describe it in terms of the customs of the time. What counts, what concerns me and all of us today, is the message that God binds himself to man by an irrevocable contract.

In this revelation at the very beginning of the Bible, at the very source of our history we find a God who gives himself to men to give them an eternal dimension. The Bible calls this commitment, this contract, the 'covenant'.

And in the rite of contract by which God binds himself to Abraham – and mankind – there is an important detail which shows movingly that God does not eliminate our freedom. The ancient ritual provided that both parties to the contract should pass through the divided animals. But here only God does. He does not make his friend Abraham do the same.

God gives his word freely and he will never retract it.

The prophets speak it in human words, it is recorded in the sacred books. Throughout the Bible, God, faithful to his word, appears as man's historical partner.

God speaks to Abraham, who is a hundred years old and he begets a people. A people is born, created – the 'people of God'. It does not matter that in reading the Bible we find that this idea of the 'chosen people', the 'people of God' takes its origin from racial pride, and that the conquest of Canaan by Joshua's tribes is, historically, merely the expression of a violent imperialism. What counts is the 'prophetic vision' – 'lift up your eyes and look' – that the biblical authors brought to their own history to see beyond the level of the sometimes very questionable events they recorded, the great hope for all mankind. . . . This is the way we should read the Bible.

We need faith to discern God's word in these very human contexts, God's word given and kept, revealing his presence in our history.

The Bible is the history of man when God makes his covenant with him.

God's covenant with Abraham gives the history of mankind its meaning. From now on a supernatural order emerges in our natural order. God speaks. He loves us and he acts. He is present in events which our freedom deforms or transforms. History now becomes a process of creation. This is what the covenant means.

Throughout the ages a 'prophetic' people is created by God and for God. And this people goes forward. It progresses painfully in its freedom and loyalty to the goal where God awaits it.

'People of God.' This includes the whole of mankind. People of flesh and blood, tormented by passions, immobilized by cowardice, heavy with sin; people of God who confess, repent, and are forgiven; a joyful people stretching out their hands towards the Lord; people in tears, afraid, at war, slaughtered; a tender people, God's beloved child; a prayerful people; a people of the earth earthy and also belonging to God; creating the Bible, their history, from man's sufferings and God's glory.

This is Israel's long march through the centuries, Israel born of the covenant. This is the march of all mankind. Until the day when God wants to come even closer to man to give himself more totally and comes down to him where he is, in flesh and blood. 'And the Word became flesh.'

Jesus came among us. And the Church, the people of God, the Church of Jesus, continues his presence among us today, a great wind of eternity blowing over our humble earth.

History goes on. Every day there are new marvels, and every further liberation of man is a leap forward towards a more total possession of the universe. But science co-ordinates phenomena, explains 'how' things are. It does not answer the question 'why' which we are eventually always brought up against – for science, for the world, for history, for our own lives.

Wars are always being waged round us and empires fall, men fight and die daily, often without even knowing why, and the oppressed can only free themselves by shedding their own blood. The Church's children, like the children of Israel long ago, keep their eyes fixed on their Father and try to discover his presence in the tormented history of the world, the history of our freedom.

This is the moment to remember the covenant. It is the only answer. 'Lift up your eyes and look.' The word given by God to Abraham in fire and blood, is still alive. It is called Jesus. And in the Eucharist which brings Christians together we still hear the words by which the God of Abraham, the God of Jesus Christ, reminds us constantly that his covenant is for ever, for better for worse.

Take, drink, this is the cup of my blood,
the blood of the new and everlasting covenant.

The covenant is man's journey to God and it is with us in our grief and in our laughter, until we reach our Father's house, the eternal dwelling place spoken of by John in the final pages of the Bible.

We see it on our desolate horizons. It stands joyful and luminous before our tired eyes:

Behold, the dwelling of God is with men.
He will dwell with them, and they shall be his people,
and God himself will be with them;
he will wipe away every tear from their eyes,
and death shall be no more,
neither shall there be mourning nor crying nor pain any more,
for the former things have passed away.   (Rev. 21.3–4)

This is the end of 'history'.

1   Cf. Jeremiah 34.18.

Recognizing a Creator God in History
THE PROPHET

Lift up your eyes and look.

If, as I believe with all my faith and try to express here, the definition involves his relationship with God and his eternal dimension, and if our God is the God of the covenant, irrevocably bound to man to fulfil his creation through him, in the liberation, reconciliation, and unity of the world, then man's vocation is to be a prophet: a witness to transcendence towards the infinite, he should try to discern the deep meaning of the events he experiences and give history its meaning. Nothing in human life is absurd or insignificant once it has a prophet.

'See.' 'Take on.' 'Go beyond': for me these words have been the keywords for freedom. The 'meaning' comes at the end. The prophet's task is to be the 'signifier'. His opposite is the meaningless man. In order to be meaningful one must be fully free.

The prophet is a man among men. He cannot step outside the life and history of his times, otherwise he is no longer a prophet. The great Bible prophets are great men of their time. They are 'present'. They are followed or they are persecuted: they are never strangers, never inaccessible, never isolated. When they come into contact with a prophet people 'become aware of themselves', they are provoked, they are involved, they are forced to interrogate themselves, they learn to know themselves better.

However, the prophet is not a 'superman'. He too is subject to sin and evil. He suffers. He knows failure and having to begin again, doubt and the overcoming of it, even rebellion sometimes, before acceptance comes. He is at odds with himself.

He is not perfect, he is not a saint. He has not developed an ideal character once and for all: he has to keep renewing his forces in order to go on with what he is doing, he has to become what he is at the cost of constant inner striving. Because he is vulnerable he gets there. . . .

He achieves this intense life and human stature because he is possessed by the 'breath of God'. He is in God's hands. We have only to reread the stories of the calling of the great prophets in the Bible (Isa. 6; Jer. 1; Ezek. 3.12–14, etc.). Their vocation appears like the irruption of the divine into their lives, an irruption that brings them to 'self'-awareness' and 'awareness of themselves for God'.

Then the whole world, creation, history, life, every event, every encounter becomes 'revelation' of God. If the prophet is 'one who speaks in the name of God' (the etymology of the word), this is because he has been taken over by God and this 'possession' gives him a new way of looking at things, so that he is able to see into the meaning of creation and the world. That is why he cannot be silent – whether he is Isaiah or Martin Luther King, Jeremiah or Helder Camara, Ezekiel or Che Guevara – and his words go beyond himself. His 'political' vision is pure and free, his political commitment is high-minded and generous.

The prophet's vision is God looking through men's eyes. This means that nothing is frivolous, everything is meaningful and speaks of God.

The prophet is 'invested' by God in both senses of the word: he is clothed by the divine presence and he is empowered to speak for God, in God's place.

He is God's familiar and is familiar with men, he addresses men in God's name, and God in the name of his brothers. He is the point of exchange. He is the sign of the covenant.

Jesus is the archetype of the prophet, the perfect encounter in his own person between man and God. He is the Chosen One, he is the Word.

Every prophet's vocation is to be a 'watchman'. This is the mission Jesus gives all who follow him when he says: 'I say to you, I say to you all: watch.' He thinks of watching as living in wait for the coming of God.

Keeping watch is one of the most common themes in the Bible. God is present and 'watches' with unending patience. He watches over man, with affection and jealousy, man his child, the crown of his creation, and man too must watch to welcome the presence of God who comes to him through each historical event.

These are the terms of the covenant. God who is love watches over man's heart which is made for loving. The relationship between God and man is between two who watch and seek each other passionately and when they have found one another they surrender to the unutterable comfort of each other's presence.

This is what prayer is: watching and waiting upon a presence. Every prophet is a witness to a God who watches over the world with love. Our God is a God who watches. He does not supervise in the name of the law. He watches in tenderness.

Every Christian – every man – because he is from God, must be a prophet among his fellows. He watches through the night. He refuses death.

He knows that our time on earth is a time of becoming, and that we must find the fair wind of God's creative breath: 'The wind blows where it wills, and you hear the sound of it, but you do not know whence it comes or whither it goes' (John 3.8).

All who watch at the bedside of the very sick, or sentries at frontline posts, know the terror of the night, the tension of waiting. This waiting sharpens all their senses and keeps them alert to the slightest rustle or whisper in the night.

They watch. They do it for others. Their presence is reassuring: it wards off danger. They are alert to threatening danger. And their hearts beating in the darkness defy death. This should be the attitude of every Christian, every free man among men.

Watching does not mean living suspiciously in a chaotic world, or living apart from other men as if they were lost souls.

Watching is keeping every sense alert to love and discerning in the beauty of the world and the dignity of man our reasons for living and hoping.

Watching means joyfully taking part in God's plan for the covenant, and seeking him everywhere.

Watching means keeping our heads held high when we suffer failure and love and life have given us bitter pain.

Watching is still believing, in spite of everything, that God does not want suffering, and that he comes to us not to explain it to us but to share it.

Watching means stretching out our sinful hands towards a God who died for sinners.

Watching means being stronger than the night, stronger

than sleep, and when it is the risen Jesus who watches in us, we are stronger than death.

We must watch. Night is all around us. The world may sleep, exhausted by its troubles. But the watcher must stand awake: he confidently awaits the dawn. We must watch: the watcher has confidence in the name of others.

And when night passes and the sky lightens in the east and the watcher sees the dawn, the world learns that it is saved. It can arise from its sleep, it can arise from death, because the sun has broken out upon all our night times, like joyful laughter after all our fears.

'Watch,' says Jesus. He reminds us of our prophetic vocation amid a tormented world. Because we also need prophets today to guard us through the night and discern among the tumult of our lives men's passionate and hungry search for the way to freedom.

We need prophets to hear God's call in the events of the day, God's sign amid the clamour of the world.

Half the world is dying of hunger. What have we done?

We need prophets, men who have risen from the dead.

We need prophets consumed by a passion for God and a passion for man. They must be convinced that all these sufferings are the birthpangs of a new world, under God's attentive care to give us confidence.

We need prophets, loving people who know from experience that the only true victory over the world is the victory of gentleness. Because such a victory is firstly a victory over oneself and a sign of freedom.

We need prophets ready to live among the sons of men as sons of God, drunk with love and freedom and who will die as the stars die in a great explosion of light to dazzle the earth. . . .

Prophets get killed. They are silenced. The meaning of history is falsified and made to conform to an ideology. Prophecy confronts the bare events. It surrenders to them. Ideology merely comments on them because this is not so risky; it can transform them and reduce them to its own measure. Prophecy proclaims the word, ideology transmits its traditions, even if these traditions suffocate the word.

Jesus tore the masks off the theologians of his day when he

told them: 'You make void the word of God through your tradition' (Mark 7.13). But there will always be other masks, and people to wear them because they are always useful.

Constantine in the fourth century was the opposite of a prophet. In Garaudy's phrase he set himself up as a 'functionary of the Absolute'. Even his conversion was ambiguous. When a Roman emperor, in the midst of a battle whose outcome is uncertain, suddenly sees a vision of the cross of Jesus and the words *In hoc signo vinces*, his conversion is not altogether convincing (and anyway, there's something wrong somewhere; this is not the way battles are won). I do not doubt the 'God of Clotilda' . . . I doubt the mystical signs given to Clovis in front of the Germans who were not a tender-hearted lot. These little miracles granted to military leaders in trouble are rather facile signs of conversion, prostitution we might say. True faith is far more costly. I know that 'Paris is worth a mass' but I do not find the Head of State's presence in Notre-Dame at national festivals, stiff and correct by his pillar in the south transept, 'prophetic'.

Unfortunately the conversion of Constantine has been taken seriously:

> Ah Constantine, what evil was the progeny not of your conversion, but the dowry the pope took from you and became wealthy. (Dante, *Hell* XIX, 115)

In this sign you shall conquer. On that day the cross of Jesus, accursed and defeated, became the standard of a victorious army. After that the popes could rule the world, and add crown upon crown as a sign of empire.

The actions of the great Bible prophets, the gospel of Jesus, and the preaching of the apostles attacked the evils of their day. After Constantine – for a long time – Christianity became the strongest bulwark of the established order. Crusaders could sack Byzantium and massacre the Albigensians: it was a 'holy war'. The Inquisition could torture the Cathars: it was purging the world of heresy. Thus the Church's mission was content to back colonialism, and Cardinal Spellman said calmly (Christmas 1966) about the Vietnam war:

> This war cannot be half-hearted . . . any other solution but victory is inconceivable. . . . The United States are the good

Samaritan of all nations. . . . They (the American soldiers) are there as soldiers of Christ, to defend the cause of justice, the cause of civilization, God's cause.

This is not the face of the Church. The prophets are to be found elsewhere. During the early centuries it wasn't Constantine, but Augustine and John Chrysostom. During the Middle Ages we do not remember Pope Innocent III, even though he was proclaimed king of kings (*rex regum*) and did a lot for the Inquisition; we think of Francis of Assisi and St Clare. In our own times we think of Pope John and his Council. . . . Cardinal Spellman is very dead.

The only prophets are those who bear witness in their lives and hearts to a personal relationship between man and God and give the best that is in them to it.

As soon as this relationship is intellectualized it becomes degraded into an ideology.

Ideology is a fudged-up reality always unable to embrace all the real conditions of real existence. Even if it does not consciously intend to deceive, at best it superimposes a redundant and useless way of talking about life, merely paraphrasing it, and at worst it sets up a barrier between life as it really is and the person who lives it.[1]

It becomes no longer a question of a 'relationship of the heart' but of 'mental assent' and the whole 'apparatus' soon gets going and with it the long procession of things that must be believed, prohibitions, excommunications, etc.

It is the death of faith.

All that remain are beliefs and they are deceptive.

I want to repeat again: the good thing about faith is God. God the creator. A loving God. All the great prophets of all time have been overwhelmed by this God. Prophets are tiring. So is the Holy Ghost. Because they are trying constantly to create the new world, to create a world 'which in part already exists where people give their lives for the sake of knowing and being, not for the sake of having'.[2]

The world cannot be created by declarations, except perhaps by this one made by a German theologian at the Second Vatican Council:

History is the only place where the Kingdom of God can be built and man is the only field for theology.

There are 'the others'.

Salvation in the Bible and the gospel is not a pious term and people who think of it as a sort of life insurance where one pays one's subscription in pious practices in this world in order to get the pay-off in the next have understood nothing at all. The word 'salvation' means 'liberation'. It implies dynamism, creation, utopia, and risk. It is never 'personal' salvation. It is the salvation of the world, the salvation of mankind. It is God's plan. He entrusted it to the freedom and courage of every person of good will.

Jesus. I see him alone with his crazy dream on the shores of Lake Galilee. He is still unknown. There are quiet boats on the lake and simple folk. It is an ordinary day; fishermen cast their nets while others sit quietly in their boats repairing broken ones. It is easy to imagine the scene. It is from the Gospel of Mark, the most human and lifelike of the gospels. Mark gives the telling details which often betray the presence of an eyewitness. He gives us a 'snapshot' of Jesus. Here he shows us Jesus looking out over the lake and even suggests what he is thinking, because suddenly the lake and the boats, the nets and the fishermen all become part of his dream, his vocation, his mission, the reason for his presence in the world which is to gather men to God and call them to create the world. So he says: 'Come, I will make you fishers of men.'

Fishers of men. This universal call has been pathetically reduced to a vocation to the priesthood as if priests alone were responsible for man's eternal destiny.

All men are responsible. And must therefore fight. Because unless he goes off the rails through the power of pride or the selfishness of ambition, what man responsible for his brothers does not commit all that he has and all that he is to struggle for their freedom, reconciliation, and unity? This is the triple challenge which has engaged the slow progress of history from the beginning and it is the sum total of Jesus's mission.

Liberation, reconciliation, unity: three words worth living and dying for. Three solemn words which challenge us, judge us, and condemn us whatever our options, opinions, or race, because we see today men, called to be sons of God, dying of hunger or in absurd wars. Because whether we belong to the right, the centre, or the left, even if good and evil are not always clearly discernible in the complications of daily issues, when we see the millions of corpses we are forced to admit our failure as human beings to care for our fellows, and we are all involved.

'I will make you fishers of men.' Let's leave aside the commentaries. These texts are not for pious souls to meditate on about 'good works'. They speak straight to our consciences. The gospel means a general call-up: it asks us to fight on all fronts for as long as there is someone or something that needs to be liberated, reconciled, or united.

Let us be clear. Even if we have not the skills or the power to resolve the tragic problems of our time, we can feel a 'common consciousness' arising in the human community in which joy and pride in the conquest of the moon, and pain and shame at massacres, are felt by all. From now on everything concerns all of us.

Even if modesty keeps us silent, selfishness wears a mask, and injustice tells lies, the great voice of silence which is the cry of the oppressed echoes through our minds in reproach.

Fishers of men. We must liberate, reconcile, unite. We must not kill or leave people to die. And today we feel more than regret, what we feel is remorse.

I too confess to a bad conscience. It is still there even though I have tried to dedicate my life to the poor. I cannot and will not get away from it. I feel part of a rich and cruel civilization of 'having', 'knowing', and 'power' which is allowing the values of 'being' quietly to die.

But I believe – this is my whole faith in man and my whole faith in God – that Jesus 2000 years ago looking out at the small group of Galilean fishermen is still looking at us in the same way today.

It is never too late to love. And it is not too late to cast the great net of God's tenderness over the world's pain. But the task is a very urgent one.

NOTES

1 Jean-Paul Dollé, *Le Désir de révolution*. Paris, Editions Grasset, p. 169.
2 Teilhard de Chardin, *The Phenomenon of Man*. London, Collins, 1959.

The Freedom of the Children of God

The creation stories define man as son of God, a creature of earth breathed upon by the divine.

The third chapter of Genesis is the story of the fall. We should not dwell upon the simple literary form of the text: it does not mean (and today we can say this without being accused of heresy) that mankind was condemned to pain, suffering, and death because of an apple stolen in a garden.

It is the story of the beginning of freedom. It still concerns the relationship between God and man, but this time from man's point of view, man in his freedom.

The human condition is essentially one of freedom. God created man uptight. Otherwise there would be no talk of a fall. Creation begins as soon as one man becomes conscious of his destiny: he will create his own history. He can accept or refuse. Anything. Accept himself or refuse himself . . . Welcome or deny his own desires. Be or have. Become or stagnate. Light or darkness. Love or hatred. Life or death. Surrender to faith or to nothingness.

He has the choice.

I remember a moment in my life, which really had nothing very dramatic about it, but which impressed me profoundly because of the meaning the occasion had for me.

I was sailing for Africa. The great ship was getting ready to leave and it was already vibrating with impatience and controlled power. Great ships are irrevocable: they cross vast oceans, days and nights, at the mercy of the waves until they reach the other unknown shore. They cross space and time.

When the last anchor is weighed and the last rope undone and the great vessel slides slowly away from the quay, it gives you a frightening feeling of finality. Your choice is set before you with great clarity as you watch the widening gap between the shore and the ship, the past and the future.

I knew what I was leaving. I knew nothing about the future except the risks I was taking.

There is only one thing to do: turn seawards. The ship's

prow is proud because it faces adventure, it faces the future, the unknown shore full of promise and threat. . . .

That day I discovered the meaning of freedom. We should be a figurehead at the prow of our own destiny, lashed by the angry sea and howling winds, driving a path through the sometimes turbulent waves, but remaining upright and directed towards the goal.

The ship 'creates' its passage. Man and all his hopes and cares are carried forward, as the sail fills with the wind and man with the breath of God.

Here we have Adam and Eve with the apple and the snake. They are about to commit an act of freedom. They will be responsible for the consequences.

They represent mankind.

Adam is not just a single man, he is mankind. Humanity did not become as it is because of Adam. On the contrary, the ancient Bible poet tells us the story of the fall because he is aware of the mystery of man and his freedom before God.

Adam is me. Sin is me. Hell is me. And the enchanting tree of knowledge – from the dream of Faust to the sorcerer's apprentice – is in my own head too.

But I am of God. And the Spirit is in me, God's breath mingled with my own. I must choose. 'To be or not to be. . . .' Adam and Hamlet are faced with the same question. And 'Sin', whose many faces are individual sins, is always concerned with this same question.

The serpent is a Canaanite divinity who reappears all over the place in the ancient Middle East. For a Hebrew author he represented the deadly foe of his God, and thus the most perfect image of evil. The serpent says to Eve: 'You will be as gods.'

This is the basis of all sinful pride, in the will to 'have', 'know', and 'be powerful'. (In the great doorway of Notre-Dame in Paris, pride is represented by a knight thrown off his horse.)

Here we have universal man forced to choose between his own finiteness and his hunger for the absolute, between his freedom and his creative power, seeking to fill some lack in himself.

Adam and Eve choose the apple and immediately find themselves in the terrifying solitude of pride, 'the wretchedness of man without God'. Thousands of years later, Pascal wrote:

Man is neither angel nor beast and his
misfortune is that when he wants to play angel
he becomes a beast.

Tragedy is what is irreversible.

And now everything is destroyed.
When men lose their joy
they also lose their life
and become merely walking corpses.

O Shade, my Light,
bright resting place for me.
Take me, take me. I want to live with you.
Not with the race of gods,
not with men who pass away.
I am no longer worthy to raise my eyes
to ask them for help.
Where can I go? Where find a safe refuge?
Because everything is collapsing, friends, everything collaps-
      ing.

Furies. Infernal goddesses.
And you, Cerberus, invincible monster
crouched at the gates through which so many dead have
      passed.
You who howl from the depths of hell,
unconquerable guardian of Hades,
King of the creatures of the night,
O Death. I invoke you,
eternal quietude. . . .   (Sophocles)

Pain, rebellion, nostalgia . . . the fall.

In Sartre's *Flies* Jupiter cries to Orestes in a final appeal:
'Who created you then, you wretch?' Orestes replies: 'You did,
but you should not have created me free.'

Before his conversion Augustine wrote: 'I sought where evil
came from and I could not get away from it. . . .' After his
baptism he discovered in man something more than human:
'Lord, you made us for yourself and our hearts are restless till
they rest in you' (*Confessions*).

In Genesis the man who feels naked after the fall and 'hides among the trees' is not Sisyphus and the God of the Bible is neither Zeus nor Jupiter. He walked in the garden and called the man: 'Where are you?'

The whole gospel in which sinners have some of the most important parts, Zaccheus, the publican, Mary Magdalene, the woman taken in adultery, the prodigal son, the Samaritan woman, the lost sheep, the good thief, echo this anxious call of God's: 'Where are you?'

And the sculptor of Chartres, with his great insight, shows us God creating Adam's face. He is thinking of Jesus . . . and God says: 'Where are you?'

Then Adam regains his freedom. History is not fatality. It has meaning. It is man's answer to his God. And Jesus comes to give it.

> . . . I am coming to thee.
> Holy Father, keep them in thy name which thou hast given
>   me,
> that they may be one, even as we are one.   (John 17.11)

The reception chapel in Notre-Dame in Paris is one of the privileged places where Adam and Eve meet after their experience with the apple tree at that dread hour of facing 'paradise lost', and nothing is left but lament, or even worse, the empty silence of a harrowed conscience, when there is nothing to be done, nothing to be said, and it is no longer a question of living but of surviving. This is the moment of decision.

Which of us in youth, or in our prime, or in old age has not suddenly been overcome by this inner silence, when the sound and the fury is suddenly stilled, when each man and woman alone surveys the life he or she has led and the life still ahead and comes up against mystery, the strength of the power to love, freedom, the absurdity of so much suffering and of death.

Then they ask the question, the only question: 'Why?' Why be born? Why live? Why must I die? What is a human being, what is love, what is freedom if they must vanish for ever into the silence of the earth?

I feel myself alive. I came into the world by the will of others, and I did not choose to be born. And I know that I carry the seeds of my own death within me. I did not choose death either. What does freedom mean on this weary road along which I stagger when I am also conditioned by country,

49

language, culture, civilization, upbringing, relationships. . . ? Who can speak of love, except as an illusion, if there is no end to carnal frailty? Because we know that the hardest suffering we can undergo is that of failing in a love relationship.

When we really stop to think of such things they weigh so heavily upon us, that our wildest passions take fright and our strength gives way.

No one is exempt, neither rich nor poor, believer nor un-believer, black nor white, because a truthful answer requires the soul to be laid bare.

I feel passionately involved and I dedicate these pages to all the men and women who have come to me at Notre-Dame, at the solemn moment in their lives when they finally lay them-selves bare. There was nothing between us but silence but in this silence I thought I could hear God's loving call to Adam when he had lost Eden: 'Where are you?'

> Man does not know where to stand, writes Pascal. He has lost his way and fallen from his right place which he cannot get back to. He seeks it everywhere with anxiety and with-out success in impenetrable darkness. . . . We want truth and find in ourselves only uncertainty. We seek happiness and find only misery and death. We are incapable of not want-ing truth and happiness, and we are capable of neither cer-tainty nor happiness. . . .[1]

Pascal goes on:

> All these miseries prove (man's) greatness. They are the mis-eries of a lord or king who has been dispossessed.[2]

I know it is possible to live a just life as an atheist: perhaps freedom is man's tragic power to confront the absurdity of his own death. . . . But death always wins.

And now I see that those who say 'God is dead' have pro-claimed the death of man with even greater finality. Because we see all the time that when people do without God they show by their dismay and anxiety their thirst for the absolute. And perhaps it is the young of today, with their rebellions and refusals, who are asking the essential questions, because above the clamour and disorder we can feel their impatience to live and the generous will to raise man to his proper level of love and freedom, to restore him to what he passionately seeks in darkness, his vocation to be God's son.

The people who walked in darkness
have seen a great light;
those who dwelt in a land of deep darkness,
on them has light shined. (Isa. 9.2)

From paradise lost, God still calls: 'Where are you?'

Something is changing. I am speaking here only from personal
experience, but I think even my humble experience of 'mankind' has some claim to universal validity. That is why I am
writing: to say about 'mankind' what I have learnt from my
experience of individuals.

Yes, something is changing: most of the men and women,
believers and unbelievers, who come to the reception chapel in
Notre-Dame, no longer come to consult a priest simply about
moral dilemmas, or how to behave, but to ask deeper questions
about how to live, what choice to make in deciding what to
become. They no longer 'submit' but 'take themselves on'.

Vocation is like freedom's eldest daughter. The meaning of
the word cannot be confined simply to what job we do, or
what state we adopt for our earthly ends. Because our state of
life, our job are only the means we choose to make something
of our lives, and lately most of the people who consult me on
this are seeking a meaning to their lives on the deepest level,
an answer to the question God asked Adam: 'Where are you?'

This means that we cannot turn immediately for answers in
moral codes or law. Our whole freedom is involved. This is
what I call 'conversion'; essentially it means taking back our
freedom into our own hands. A recent debate with Francis
Jeanson brought up this word. Francis Jeanson does not like
Christian vocabulary. I told him that neither of us liked what
habit, routine, and stupidity had turned Christian vocabulary
into: a caricature.

And anyway, the word 'conversion' is not confined to Christian vocabulary and I have often met unbelievers who have
been converted to something other than Christianity. Self-
discovery or rediscovery, self-conquest or reconquest, moving
from habit to the creation of a new self, taking on rather than
submitting, mastering a situation which previously controlled
us, are the essential steps towards conversion. Conversion is
the desire to become 'more' than we already are. It is being

faithful to oneself. Becoming aware of 'who I am' in order to become 'who I should'. And if conversion involves breaking away, this is a breaking away from all the forms of alienation, even the subtlest ones, that up till then had prevented me from becoming myself. True conversion is permanent.

> It lifts him who dares out of the peaceful, busy life in which lie selfishness and attachment . . . we must leave our peace and rest and abandon them constantly to create better forms for our work, art, and thought. To stop and enjoy is a sin against action. We must always be pressing on, surpassing ourselves and leaving our favourite attainments behind us.[3]

What Teilhard de Chardin wrote about creation is even truer of conversion, which is indeed self-creation.

And Francis Jeanson who does not like the word conversion speaks of it very well when he comments favourably on Sartre's idea that it is necessary to 'betray ourselves': '. . . betray in ourselves precisely that which cuts us off from ourselves'.[4] 'Vocation and freedom', 'conversion and freedom' . . . I'd like to add 'confession and freedom'.

Here too something is changing. Confession has at last stopped being the wretched routine where a pathetic list of sins was mumbled in the dark, always the same sins awaiting the formula of absolution. People used to go to confession like doing the washing. The absurd prisonlike confessional box is falling into disuse: the vast majority of Christians I meet prefer confession face to face, as more dignified and truthful.

Isaiah the prophet writes: 'Do not remember the past. Do not think of it any more. "Behold, I am making a new world," says God.' These are the words of reconciliation sought by Christians who come to confession. First to still their anxiety, relieve their remorse, and drown the grief of the memory of the many betrayals we have on our consciences.

'Behold, I am making a new world.' This does not mean wiping out the past or eliminating our experiences. Only free men are capable of accepting their past, whatever it may have been, not to be dominated by it but to recognize and accept it and make sense of it for the future. My past is mine. My past is me. Every moment of my life has gone to making me what I am.

Whatever our failures, betrayals, disappointments, even if

we have destroyed everything or messed everything up, we can still look up humbly and find in God the Father's loving kindness, the new world he offers us to make a success of our lives.

Making a success of our lives sometimes means accepting the unacceptable, transforming day by day with untiring confidence and obstinate rebeginnings the bad into the good, the negative into the positive, taking pride in what might make us feel disgraced, and destroying the memory of evil by an 'excess of faithfulness'. We can never start our lives again. We have to go on with them. Starting again from scratch means flight from ourselves.

We have to go on to build again on ruins, this is what 'being free' means. This is the way I think God sees our past.

Paul echoes this thought in his letter to the Philippians:

> One thing I do, forgetting what lies behind and straining forward to what lies ahead, I press on toward the goal. . . . (Phil. 3.13)

'Forgetting what lies behind' does not mean denying our lives. It means refusing to let our past block our future. Then the past is no longer a burden we have to carry again every morning when we wake up, the heavy weight of all our sins and remorse.

Paul like Isaiah sees the past as a joyful movement towards an optimistic God who opens his arms to us to transform our disappointments, betrayals, bitterness, and weariness and embraces us as we are, to go on creating us for joy.

Having been is not enough. Being what we are is not enough. We must keep growing. We must go on step by step towards the goal. Perhaps our pace will not always be a steady one, but that's not the point, as long as we walk freely in God's sight with every confidence that by the very act of setting out on this journey we are saved.

I think this is one of the most important meanings of confession. We do not go to confession to 'root out' the evil which hurts and humiliates us, like pulling out a bad tooth. We go to confession to 'take on' our past, to reclaim it and offer it to God's mercy.

NOTES

1   Pascal, *Pensées*. Lafuma, 400–401; 116.
2   Ibid.
3   Teilhard de Chardin, *Etre plus*. Paris, Editions du Seuil, p. 83.
4   Francis Jeanson, *Sartre dans sa vie*. Paris, Editions du Seuil, p. 287.

'The Sound of Consciences . . .'

More and more today, the men and women who ask to see a priest want to see him on this level of freedom.

It is a reassuring trial, and I am proud to be able to bear witness to it. More and more, our contemporaries are acquiring a taste for 'being oneself'. A life's mistakes are now being seen as 'failures to be' (there it is, *the* sin!), infidelities to oneself, and no longer just individual offences against an external law. Not at all that the law has come to be held in derision, as people are sometimes too quick to say when the only principle of their lives is 'order'. Law is not 'secondary' – it is 'second'. The first thing is freedom. Law is at the service of liberties, to convoke, provoke them, to point them in directions where it is possible to become. Freedom gives law its highest meanings and sometimes changes them. Freedom studs its path with laws, like a climber, clinging to the face, who puts in the crampons which will help him to climb.

It is fortunate that in a time like ours nothing and no one can throw off this powerful pressure for liberation. Nothing can resist the will to be and to become, once – and it need only be once – it has been caught by a conscience.

Art, that criterion which searches in the boldest forms, colours, and dissonances for an expression of man freed from the mud in which our society has got bogged down, art separates itself from us, but only to summon us. Don't go and tell young modern artists that they disappoint us. Our very disappointment sets the seal on their will to create a new world.

'I'm coming to think more and more,' writes Van Gogh, 'that we shouldn't judge God by this world. It's one of his studies that didn't come off.'

It makes sense, in this vast murmur of awakened consciences, that the decision of a man or woman to see a priest should no longer be prompted by morality or devotion. They don't come for 'words of comfort'. However little their souls are free, they reject soothing consolations, and anyone who takes his life in his hands prefers the harshness of a brutal truth if it is the truth for *him*. He won't let anyone hide misfortune from him if misfortune has burst into his life; he won't let anyone anaesthetize him with words if the words are going to hide anything of his destiny.

Men and women are anxious. They are looking for the escape towards the Absolute who could break their solitude and open their prisons.

They have built great structures glowing with colour and light, but we know that the people who live there know nothing about each other: they have made collectivities when they should have made fraternal communities.

I think of the feverish crowd in our great city of Paris. Each morning it pours into the tunnels of the Métro. In the sickly fluorescent glow they all run like hunted people. They run. Pursued by anxiety and launched towards anguish. All those faces impassive as masks. You look for human glances, but most of the time you only find faces closed, fixed, and distorted by some inward drama. Ulcers of the soul.

We condemn violence in the name of the best principles without seeing that it too is a cry of despair, because all that the people who kill each other lack is a reason to hope and believe in their brothers.

In the name of morality we condemn the bursts of eroticism which have suddenly unhinged our time, without seeing that these excesses are only the longing of a world greedy for love, for a love which no one can give any more.

People are anxious, and when anxiety brings them to God, it is to face the ultimate question of their destiny. And that is already the beginning, the threshold of faith.

I want to quote here a very beautiful piece from Francis Jeanson in his book on Sartre. It is perhaps one of those points of convergence between what he calls his 'unbeliever's faith' and my faith as a son of God.

> . . . all belief is a taking for granted of the Absolute. Faith, on the other hand, tries to be absolute simply on the level of its own risk, its own stand, its own commitment, that is, in its very way of accepting the 'relative'. A believer abandons himself to an endless relativism. One belief is as good as another; each appeals directly to the theologians' Incommunicable, Ineffable, Unutterable.
>
> The man of faith, in contrast, commits himself totally only

to allow himself to be totally tested by others and by events. His conviction is relatively absolute because in it he puts at risk even the meaning of his own existence, but it is 'absolutely relative' because from the start he has chosen to measure truth by his own power to make it come about. Belief is a taking for granted of truth; faith is a demand for meaning. The believer defines himself *against* unbelief or other beliefs; the man of faith can only confirm 'his' faith by recognizing it at work in the most radical demand of any man.[1]

A priest counsellor is not what used to be called a 'duty priest', responsible for administering rites.

A priest counsellor's responsibility is serious. Those who come to him rarely have a clear view of their situation. Often the disappointment of a life which has failed to live up to its promises, humiliation and bitterness at happiness destroyed, the diffused pain which comes from a scattered self, and being unused to exploring one's own mystery, all this contributes in advance to laying traps in the conversation.

Timid, clumsy language is therefore going to betray resurgences of belief. In this difficult moment of life, with no other support in putting oneself into words than the memories of days gone by and the pitiful vocabulary of past lessons, a person sees the priest as someone to fall back on, as a refuge. He is on the other bank. He is well in with this God whom one has lost, and who, one remembers, sometimes answers. That's the trap.

If the priest in front of him is no more than a churchman – be he an excellent man – possessor of truth (including his visitor's); if he is the infallible oracle, the officer of the Absolute, armed with dogmas, principles, and laws; if his competence is limited to moral theology, judgement, ritual; if he projects himself, often unconsciously, with his certainties, however noble, and his difficulties, however heroic; if he prefers to advise; if he tries to 'win back' the other person; if he is the authority who already knows, before the other person, what should be done; if he applies the laws, even with compassion: if he does all this, the trap closes and it's still alienation.

They will part happy with each other, one because he will have 'saved a soul', the other because he is going away warmly wrapped in belief. But his self is not involved. Only his behaviour is affected. It has been a failure.

Now very often, through the clumsy language of a person who is trying to put his whole self into words, one must try to recognize the person speaking. In this self-accusation, even if it is generous, in which a creature is freeing itself of its burden, there is always an emotional climate in which confusion, suffering, and bitterness have swallowed up the speaker. He unburdens himself, sometimes with the shamelessness of despair. One has to listen and listen again. And bury oneself in that distress. The priest who knows how to listen is no longer confronting a misfortune; he is inside it. It is at this level of communion that he will be able to read, in that suffering face turned towards him, a destiny being sought. The task is to listen, listen humbly, all faculties alert, and wait for a sign of that pure spring which still flows even in the depths of devastated consciences.

What human problem, moral, social, political, or religious, is not first of all a problem of freedom?

And what good does it do to suggest an act of faith if it is understood as a new constraint, more noble perhaps, but external to oneself? Even if such an act can strangle other forms of slavery for a time, it is not free, and if it does not involve the whole person it will be another form of alienation, and certainly not an act of faith.

Freedom must be set free. That is the essential mission of all those who, by their vocation, their profession, or simply by their personal influence, are called to help their brothers. In the order of faith I dare to say this because I have seen it: to set freedom free is to set free the Spirit, who is present in the hearts of all men.

What new excellence can one call a man to if he has not first accepted himself? And how can he accept himself if he has never seen himself, never possessed himself? What truth can he claim if he is not first true to himself?And what is truth to oneself if one has never become aware of oneself? This is the beginning of all freedom. I think it is also the beginning of all holiness.

In the Bible, to save is to set free.

In any meeting – here I am thinking especially of that of a priest with his brothers, since that is my life, but I am not making that the only case, or a criterion, or even the most important – in any meeting the will to liberate should take precedence over judgement and condemnation.

Jesus, in his dealings with the Pharisees, wise men, doctors, lawyers, and theologians of his time, rejects this segregation in which men claiming to be pure, but swollen with pride and contempt, reject their brothers.

He refuses to judge because to judge a man is to freeze him, to petrify him in his state when one judges him. It is to block him in his becoming and to doubt his possibilities.

My ministry has taken me to meet prisoners in their cells, and prostitutes and vagrants in the disturbed nights of Pigalle.

What makes prisoners suffer is not just the punishment inflicted on them by a court, but more especially the permanent character of the judgement which society passes on them and which they have to bear all their lives like a birthmark. A murderer is not just a murderer; but when he has finished his sentence and the moment comes to rejoin the human community, he is still forced to read in all eyes that the judgement remains.

I remember Pigalle. Father Talvas, who has devoted all his priestly life to the liberation of prostitutes, had let me join his team for a while, and I tried to be what he himself has been for thirty years in the midst of degradation: a sign of hope.

I walked the pavements of Pigalle, all my senses alert. I was there to be the presence of Jesus Christ risen without knowing how that presence would one day become visible.

To be the one recognized by his footstep, the friend. Faced with those girls who called to me, I felt no contempt but, on the contrary, a great wave of tenderness.

I was on the side of the poor, on that level of wretchedness where the world of other people can't hurt any more because there is nothing more to expect, nothing more to lose. The good people have left the prostitutes on the lowest level of degradation. They talk about them with pity, ridicule, or contempt.

And still I went to Pigalle to meet the Spirit who is present everywhere, in all, to try to show in the offer of friendship that it is always possible to love and be free. To try to reveal to a prostitute that she can become what she is, first and foremost a woman, and that she still carries in herself the beauty of the world.

I may well be charged with naivety – what do I care! It is enough for me to have seen those tired faces and deadened eyes light up in a moment of happiness and reveal a beauty which had seemed dead, intact treasures buried under contempt, as though the excess of loneliness and suffering had protected them.

I became aware that I was part of a society which has not yet accepted the poor. It tolerates them.

All would be saved if the well-to-do felt themselves wounded by the poverty of the poor.

The conversations which I was able to start up with the prostitutes and vagrants sometimes led me to the very limit of poverty, even more tragic than material want: poverty of being.

To come to grips with this poverty one has first to accept a total dispossession of oneself, since even the most humble words are too rich to get through to such abasement. When the prostitute is walled in by an irrevocable loneliness, when intelligence has slowly been suffocated in the darkness of want and distress, when her eyes have never known any other horizon than the most appalling injustice. This is indeed to be born for unhappiness if no tenderness has ever brushed that impassive face, set against its night; the heart quietly closes, the spirit goes out, the sensibility hardens, and the human person slowly sinks into the ooze of degradations, beyond contempt, even beyond despair. Nothing more can touch her: she looks on the happiness of others as another world in which she is not involved.

Prostitution is not even shameful any longer because the only voice which can still sound in her darkened conscience is that of revolt or, alternatively, despair, the sneer or the scream.

Poverty of being. . . .

Some find relief in it, because the peace of the wretched is the fact that they no longer need to fight because they have nothing more to save – not even hope:

> The wretch is alone in his wretchedness, says Péguy, and the constant look he casts on his wretchedness is a wretched look. . . . Wretchedness is not one part of his life; it is a slavery with no remission. It is not just the procession of privations, maladies, dreariness, despair, ingratitude and death –

it is a living death, the universal penetration of death into life. And for the wretch death is only the consummation of defeat, the consummation of despair.   (Jean Coste, *Péguy*)

The humblest and most insignificant of us is a cherished child of God. And the person who has been humiliated, dishonoured, brought low among his fellows, he above all is waiting for a 'presence' which will finally break down his loneliness and restore him to himself, and give him back, with a little friendship, a reason to live, to hope, to be free, and to love.

He is not waiting for compassion. To be compassionate may be to judge with great kindness, but it is still 'judging'. He is not waiting for our advice. He knows it all. He is not waiting for our words of consolation. They would not touch him. One needs only to have suffered to know that silence soothes more than words when it reveals the presence of a friend.

He is waiting for someone who will share, who will be willing to descend with him to the deepest level of his humiliation. . . . 'Go and find your brother,' says the gospel, 'and if he listens to you, you have gained your brother.'

Yes, go and find your brother, and let him understand by one glance from your eyes that he will never be alone again. Go and find your brother and say to him, 'Look up. With your sin, you are here in front of me like my own mirror image. I am not pure enough to bring you forgiveness, but I am poor enough to beg for it with you. Your love is in tatters, your freedom is trapped; you are as like to me as a brother, for my tenderness is fragile and my freedom is unsteady. Come, we will combine my hope and your sin and fight together.'

This is perhaps the profound truth of every confession.

The confessor and his penitent are united by the same movements of flesh and blood. They are united by the same moments of weariness. United by sin. United above all, and mingled by the tenderness of the same Father and the pardon which goes from one to the other, wraps them together, and brings them to that high level of faith, humility, and charity where one no longer knows who forgives and who is forgiven.

'You have no excuse . . . when you judge another; for in passing judgment upon him you condemn yourself. . . .' (Rom. 2.1).

I have witnessed crimes and violations of conscience which

can sometimes be committed with the sickening gentleness of compassion when it judges (and I too who write these lines) – as if kindness gave a right to judge. As if my pretended moral rectitude could be a criterion in the face of another's tragedy. Worthless counsellors who contemplate themselves as they project their virtue on to the other. Even if their judgement ends in forgiveness, they have judged, and in that very attitude they place themselves 'over against' the other person and 'above' him; it's already a lie. And even if they are right about the Law, even if their compassion is moving, they are wrong to be right like that. Laws are general, cases are particular.

Principles are always simple, situations complex. That is why a rigid defender of principles is always a false accuser.

The father of the prodigal son, in Luke's Gospel, doesn't ask his son questions. He interrupts him when he starts accusing himself, and brings the ring, the tunic, and the fatted calf to do him honour. Such is the disproportion of forgiveness when it comes from God.

We must hurry to restore the other person to himself, to give him his freedom, before we give the subtle hints of judgement a chance to creep in.

Jesus, faced with the adulterous woman, firmly opposed the judgement even of the Law.

The Jewish law was formidable: any woman proved guilty of adultery was immediately tried and sentenced to death. She died by stoning. Guilty husbands, it is true, were not treated in the same way, but attitudes in the ancient world were far from giving a woman the place she has – or could have – in our society.

Here, Jesus is being hunted. A band of fanatical Pharisees surrounds him. Judges. The trap is set. Jesus can forgive, but then he enters into open hostility with the Law, the holy, sacred law, the law of Moses, which required the death penalty. Or he can hand the adulterous woman over to her executioners, but then he is on the side of the judges, and contradicts his message of love. We are in complete suspense, and can feel the tension in the silence.

Faced by these men driven by hatred, sure of their principles, faced by this humiliated and terrorized woman, faced by the inevitable onlookers, Jesus maintains a sovereign calm.

His idle finger mechanically traces a few signs in the dust. He frees himself from the threat: the trap will close on air. Any man capable of meeting the violence of passions with that admirable serenity immediately sets himself above the debate. Jesus refers the judges to their own consciences: 'Let him who is without sin among you cast the first stone.'

Immediately, the tense silence becomes an embarrassed silence. And Jesus goes back to writing in the dust. He too is sure of himself. One by one, the accusers withdraw. The gospel has not left out the little touch of humour in the ending. They go away 'one by one', inconspicuously, beginning with the oldest, the most burdened consciences. . . .

Then Jesus looks at the adulterous woman. He doesn't preach at her. He doesn't load her with reproaches. He doesn't give her advice. He doesn't even use the enormous power he's just acquired over her. He doesn't judge her. It's easy to imagine his smile, full of tenderness: he reconciles her, he restores her to herself, he offers her the renewal which is in all liberation. 'Go and sin no more.' It is not that Jesus minimizes this woman's sin. (One sometimes hears people using this text to relativize their betrayals.) Jesus does not deny the sin, but he refuses to imprison man in his sin. He shows him the escape route which will set him free and give him back all his possibilities.

His attitude illustrates one of the fundamental aspects of the gospel:

> For God sent the Son into the world, not to condemn the world, but that the world might be saved through him. (John 3.17)
>
> The Father judges no one. (John 5.22)
>
> You judge according to the flesh, I judge no one. (John 8.15)
>
> Judge not and you will not be judged. (Luke 6.37)

To judge a man, even for his greater good, to condemn him for his past, his sin, is always to lie, because we never know the secrets of a heart, the anguish of its struggles, the sadness and the pain of its failures. In the prostitutes of Pigalle, when it was possible to reach the human person they hide under their make-up and still protect jealously in the depths of their loneliness, I have encountered all the springs of tenderness, freshness, and respect which are the beauty of every woman.

To judge is to tailor a freedom to our measurements, to cut away possibilities it always has hidden within it. A freedom regained is often the gift of miracles.

'I do not even judge myself,' Paul told the Corinthians.

And it does indeed often happen that the judgement a man passes on himself dissolves for ever the will to create himself again, whereas so often, in the passion which unbalances him, in the very vice which humiliates him, there are hidden streams which, if they were tapped, would reveal to him deep springs of great richness.

He has put himself into a moral state, discouraged before trying. He has examined himself before the Law. The Law has fallen like the axe, forcing from him the final 'yes' or 'no'.

If he examined himself before himself, he might discover that the 'no' he has opposed to his own becoming is not absolute: running through it are unexpressed regrets, longings, and hopes which are waiting tensions. His freedom, in him, is always lying in wait. There are thus refusals which, like some sores which itch when nearly healed, swarm with living germs of acceptance.

There are passions whose power must be tapped. And some sorts of despair are fed by the same springs as hope. And we need to be clear about the glittering movement of our own consciences. Jesus lets the tares grow in the field; he knows that the good seed is there, and that it too is alive. We are unfinished creatures, but constantly 'mobilized' by creative power. The judgement on oneself in which a man paralyses himself, just as a photo freezes movement, whether through ignorance, weariness, laziness, or discouragement, always dams creative freedom. We are still being made.

Here again, the act of faith is liberating: if it isn't regarded as a utilitarian recipe or a moral attitude, but is a living relation, personal and trusting, with a God who saves, a God who loves me as I am and not as I used to dream of being. The act of faith, by transcending the shadowy areas in which we were in danger of imprisoning ourselves, liberates the creative movement. Then everything is possible. One can dream one's life.

I believe that the parable of the sower which the gospel

records (Matt. 13.3–9) is this optimistic message in which Jesus reveals to us a God who saves, whatever happens. The point of the story is the final harvest, and Jesus's insistence on the difficulty of the sowing is simply to highlight by contrast the joy of the harvest: 'Other seeds fell on good soil and brought forth grain, some a hundredfold, some sixty, some thirty.' In spite of all the obstacles.

The attitude of the sower who sows his seed on the rocky ground, on the paths, or among the thorns is not surprising. In that period fields were sown before being ploughed, and the sower would go round the stubble-fields throwing his seed around him, even on the temporary path, on the thorn-bushes or the stones, which would be ploughed in after he had passed. There was enough good soil in his field to make up for the seed wasted on the barren areas, and that was what mattered.

In the same way, Jesus wants to remind us that the world and the heart of man have been sown with divinity, and that, even if we have within us areas of dryness, clay, or areas which choke the word of God, the promise of the harvest will be kept. We are saved.[2]

So true is this that Jesus proclaims results which far exceed reality. We know that in that period a tenfold yield was a very good harvest. A sevenfold or fivefold yield was normal. Jesus proclaims a yield of thirty-, sixty-, a hundredfold. This is the boundlessness of God's tender love for man.

So, we may be disappointed by life every day, may accumulate failures, may be crushed by suffering, but the parable of the sower tells us that we are created to 'become', and that, even from beginnings without hope, the result is achieved, and it is magnificent.

Yes, anything is possible. There are no failed lives. There is no bitterness without hope. We must passionately refuse to freeze a situation by judging it.

You who were my love and my joy, you have become my anger and my bitterness. But what does suffering matter, since if your heart has been choked in the thorns or dried up on the stony path, I know that the sower has sown our hope; I shall carry it into the night, and soon, soon, we shall rise together, in the blinding light of the first tender stirrings, and we shall reap our eternal joy.

That too is the parable of the sower. At the limit of patience, on the other side of suffering, there is joy, and the radiant face of a God who saves.

This is what the Bible means when it sings in the psalms:

He that goes forth weeping,
bearing the seed for sowing,
shall come home, with shouts of joy,
bringing his sheaves with him.   (Ps. 126.6)

NOTES

1   Francis Jeanson, *Sartre dans sa vie*. Paris, Editions du Seuil, p. 269.

2   I deliberately do not refer to the explanation of the parable of the sower given in the same chapter of Matthew's Gospel. Most exegetes regard this as a later addition by the primitive Church which no longer stresses the main message of the story, the harvest.

Faith and Freedom

Once it comes from within, from the very springs of one's 'sense of oneself', once it is experienced on the same register as the life force, the relation of man to God becomes truth to self, and catalyses all energies in order to direct them towards the 'greater than self'. It is this tension which never ceases to stimulate consciousness to transcend itself in order to reach the dimension of eternity which it has recognized as its being. It is this tension which, as time goes on, will break all the fastenings and all the alienations which impede the proud and powerful movement towards 'surplus being'.

Faith is freedom.

And if, in a second movement, it accepts the lines of reflection offered to it, it does so because it has first recognized them as 'truth to self'.

If it accepts rites, it is in order to spread out in 'celebration' of what it is constantly living.

Besides, the lines of reflection – the expressions of revelation, the theological tradition – were invented by faith. The rites – prayer, the sacraments – are also second to faith, and only nourish it if faith recognizes itself in them, so much so that it constantly reinvents them since, like any lived relation, faith is a permanent discovery and questioning.

Any progression towards 'surplus being' is a new demand to 'be more', to go from the 'conscious' to the 'lived' and from the 'lived' to the 'celebrated'. What shapes a man is 'in front'; in the act of faith he can lose himself in giving himself, and find himself again completely.

'He who loses his life saves it,' says Jesus, and I want to take that paradoxical saying as the charter of my freedom.

At this point one would need to quote all the passages of the Old and New Testaments which would show the development and refinement of the concept of freedom to the same degree that the relation of man to God becomes a deep personal intimacy.

The spirit you received is not the spirit of slaves bringing fear into your lives again; it is the spirit of sons, and it makes us cry out, 'Abba, Father!'   (Rom. 8.15, JB)

The main heralds of Christian freedom are Paul and John. This would be the place for a commentary on Paul's letter to the Galatians:

When Christ freed us, he meant us to remain free. . . . My brothers, you were called, as you know, to liberty.   (Gal. 5.1, 13, JB)

John regarded the act of faith as the source of all freedom:

. . . the truth will make you free. . . . So if the Son makes you free, you will be free indeed.   (John 8.32, 36, JB)

Liberation from sin, which is the refusal to 'be more' and so the principle of all alienation.

Liberation from death, the implacable spectre, the absurd and violent contradiction of the generous tension of any freedom to 'invent life'.

Liberation from the law, because the law is external to me, and the movement which rises out of the hidden depths of my consciousness is greater than the law and transfigures it. My obedience to the law is buried in my truth to myself, to the other person, to all others.

Here freedom reaches the peak of man's 'signification'. Right at the end of transcendence he bares himself 'for others', his vision opens to the universal, he is 'responsible', and his freedom is fulfilled in charity.

Paul writes:

For you were called to freedom . . .; only do not use your freedom as an opportunity for the flesh, but through love be servants of one another.   (Gal. 5.13)

Faith, freedom, charity, three beautiful sprays of light which are man's splendour. They spring from the same inner furnace which devours every man hungry for transcendence, who 'becomes-what-he-is' by leaping generously towards the 'greater-than-himself'.

Ah, what is man that you should spare a thought for him, the son of man that you should care for him? Yet you have made him little less than a god.   (Ps. 8.4–5, JB)

John and Paul take this view of man to the infinite, both transfigured by the revelation of his destiny: 'We are of God,' says John, and Paul exclaims, 'We are of his race.'

In the first letter of Paul to the Corinthians there is a short passage which, even if not written specifically as a definition of freedom, nevertheless illuminates particularly well the attitude of the free man as he searches for the necessary harmony between the worries, the joys, the sufferings of daily life, and the demands of the interior life, between the reality of our carnal world in which everyone attempts to fulfil himself with the gifts he has received and in spite of his limitations, and that other reality which is the presence in the world of a God who is a creator.

> I mean, brethren, the appointed time has grown very short; from now on, let those who have wives live as though they had none, and those who mourn as though they were not mourning, and those who rejoice as though they were not rejoicing, and those who buy as though they had no goods, and those who deal with the world as though they had no dealings with it.   (1 Cor. 7.29–31)

These words, typical of Paul's frequently contrasting style, may well appear paradoxical, and there will always be disappointed minds, embittered consciences, and narrow systems of thought which will read into them an austere rule supposedly teaching contempt for all earthly joy, suspicion of the happiness of life, as though flowers were not meant to be picked, music and painting were not meant to enchant us, the love of a man and a woman was no longer to be celebrated, as though life hadn't been given to us to be lived.

On the contrary, it is a text full of optimism, wisdom, and health, and Paul presents, in a few well-shaped phrases, the Christian's moral law: he has the right to use joyfully the good things of this world, while always taking care not to let himself be imprisoned by them.

Paul suppresses neither joy nor sadness. He knows that the little community in Corinth must no longer be a slave of the riches and the passions which flooded into the great city, and from that point the words he addresses to it have taken on a universal dimension, have echoed through the centuries and reach us today, in the middle of a consumer society in which, as we see daily, the lure of profit threatens to crush human dignity.

Let those who deal with the world act as though they had no dealings with it.

Here again, freedom sheds light on life. And in the tempestuous times in which we live, in which people are so quick to confuse independence with freedom, this text of Paul's is crucial.

He reminds us that the only freedom is the freedom of one's self, and that a man is only free if he is greater than his greatest passion, richer than his dearest treasure, nobler than his noblest certainty.

He teaches us that the values of having are at the service of the values of being, profit is at the service of man, and that it is more important to 'live successfully' than to 'succeed in life'.

'Let those who deal with the world act as though they had no dealings with it.' It is not a matter of denying the world or mutilating life, but only of understanding that 'well-being' must never compromise the drive towards 'more being', and that, if he wants to keep his power to love, any Christian – and man of good will – must learn to master the power of money, to dominate the stirrings of fleshly passion.

This is the role of freedom.

Sometimes, at a turning of life, freedom appears in full light, dazzling and fascinating, and challenges us and touches us at that hidden point of ourselves where each of us knows that there are no other answers than to look at oneself. It penetrates us like a blade, eliminating all pretexts, all alibis, all hesitations. We know, once and for all, what there is left for us to do, whatever the cost, and any man who has once met his own freedom can never again close his eyes to the demand to which it summoned him. He then either takes up the struggle or resigns himself to living unhappily.

It is freedom which crosses our path at the moment of important choices, to make us pull off the last masks and accept the truth, even if the truth is cruel.

'The truth will make you free,' said Jesus (John 8.32).

Freedom. Each of us can recognize it. It is 'that face which resembles us like a brother and comes towards us in a mirror', with the question, simply with the question, 'Who are you? Where are you going?'

Freedom is often the sister of solitude, since no one can come with us in the secret arguments into which she leads us.

Independence is arrogance when it doesn't accept limits or constraints. Freedom recognizes them, accepts them, transcends them, and it is in this movement in which she thrusts us to the tip of ourselves that she is the most faithful servant of love.

Independence does what it wants: so much the worse for the law and so much the worse for others.

Freedom does what it has to. It is never 'in breach of the law', even if sometimes its demands take us 'beyond the law'.

The advice Paul gives to his little community in Corinth reminds us simply that we are children of God, meant to live free and to love.

Elsewhere, in his letter to the Romans, he widens his view: he sees the whole of creation, nature, and life which have been entrusted to us, subject to our whims, and waiting for their own liberation.

> The whole creation is eagerly waiting for God to reveal his sons . . . creation still retains the hope of being freed, like us, from its slavery to decadence, to enjoy the same freedom and glory as the children of God.   (Rom. 8.19, 21, JB)

We see it clearly today, and the statistics are getting worrying: by exhausting nature just to provide profit, we have disfigured it and sometimes butchered it. It was the glory of man to have detected the prodigious forces nature carries within it. They were given to us to complete the world and make life a song. We made bombs to kill.

Today we have shattered the silence, polluted the springs and the rivers, and even the birds of the air and the fish of the sea can no longer be happy. What was joy has become a threat.

We were created to spread life, proud to be building a new world. And there is war.

Millions and millions of children die of hunger. And nature, so beautiful and so gentle, nature is dying slowly at our hands. Must the sons of God become ministers of death and reign over ruins? Must we be ashamed to be human?

A man who has a wife and makes her an object of his use and his pleasure destroys his wife. Paul tells us, 'Let the man who has a wife behave as though he had no wife.'

If someone is suffering and no one helps him to win his freedom to come through the test, he will sink into revolt and despair. Paul tells us, 'Let the person who mourns live as though he were not mourning.'

If someone has found pleasure and joy, and he is not greater than his own happiness and can spread it, he will slip into egoism and destroy his own happiness. Paul tells us, 'Let the person who rejoices live as though he was not rejoicing.'

This is the role of freedom. And Paul knows well that it is fragile: 'We carry our treasures in vessels of clay,' he said.

And it is true. All it takes is a bit too much well-being, a bit too much wealth, and freedom is threatened. All it takes is one taboo, one unrestrained passion, and we are slaves to the worst of slaveries, slaves to ourselves.

And even if the passion is deliberate, willed, and conscious. Is one freer because one has chosen one's prison?

Freedom is not a result. It is a tension, a wanting, a becoming, a permanent creation. One is never free. One is freeing oneself.

Freedom makes us fighting men. With all that fighting implies: failures, victories, great bursts of generosity, moments of enormous weariness, now shouts of joy, now sobs.

The main task, here, is to endure.

Until that wonderful day, the day of the resurrection, when we see the new world opening to us, our own death defeated, and discover together the fullness of freedom and with it the fullness of life.

Yes, 'when Christ freed us, he meant us to remain free'. And that is a task to perform. And it includes creating the world, creating man, creating life.

Flashes

One day I walked on and on through the bush and got lost. Suddenly I came across a single hut in a clearing hidden by trees. A hut in the sunshine with a huge, half naked black man standing in front of it: his face was rugged and his muscles rippled under his glistening skin. He was working on a piece of wood with a matchet. I asked him the way. He gave a loud disconcerting scream: 'E-e-e-e-kie!' Then he turned to the hut and barked out some rapid, brutal phrase with the resonance of a tom-tom. At once a small girl appeared in the doorway. She was carrying a spear and passed it to the huge man without a word. 'Nkelek,' he said, 'let's go' . . . and we set out.

I gazed at the magnificent giant. He crashed through the high, stiff, swaying grass. Methodically he cut his way through the undergrowth with his matchet, holding his lance in his left hand. Sometimes he looked up and sniffed, he was literally smelling out the way. Instinctively he came to terms with the wilderness. His matchet cut us a path. All his gestures were very fine but I was especially impressed by his dark eyes intent on his task.

This powerful man silently cutting through the undergrowth, mysterious in his coloured loincloth, bounding ahead of me with supple catlike strides, was inseparable from the forest. He gave the forest a soul and the strange vibrations which united him with it were quite alien to me. I was a stranger in the forest. He was at home. He had a knowledge I had not, a culture of which I was completely ignorant, and the great growing silence engulfing us was like a familiar creature to him, whose movements he knew, whereas for me it was a mystery.

In this concert between man and cosmos I recognized a work of art, and the forest man was not a rustic in his communion with the forest.

We walked in silence.

The tall grasses fell beneath his shining blade. They wavered for a moment, then yielded and the cut stalks with their wet and shining wounds were a note of freshness beneath the torrid sky.

At last a final cut revealed the track. My guide went home, smiling broadly. He raised his blade towards the narrow path open before us under the trees leading to silence.

We parted.

I spent ten years in the great South Cameroon forest and I took part in the exciting work of bringing the Church to birth there. My first reaction when I arrived, in 1953, was one of stupor. From the very beginning I felt worried because my training had prepared me to give, to give everything: what I had, what I was, my culture, my heart, my ideas, my health, my faith. I had not been trained to receive.

I had arrived in a new world with different people, a different race. Unknown treasures, about which I had been told nothing, awoke new vibrations in me, expressing the universal language of mankind; a language of rhythm and music, an astonishing collection of proverbs expressing the wisdom of a people, ancestral customs and sacred rites, in which water, blood, and fire were the chief symbols, as in the Bible.

I had come to teach and from the very beginning I realized that I had everything to learn, to assimilate this wealth belonging to 'mankind' which we Europeans had completely disregarded.

People had told me about Africa and the 'poor black people' with such great compassion that I felt betrayed by these splendours.

I was a priest in the Church of Jesus Christ and possessed all the wealth of my own country's culture and my faith; but when I heard the delirious rhythm of the tom-tom and saw dancers fall into a trance beneath the moon, or heard the stories sung in the evening round the fire, and even when I saw the dark rite in which the witch-doctors confronted the powers of evil, my proud culture which, as a Westerner, I assumed to be the height of human development and had brought here as a magnificent gift, suddenly seemed very lacking.

Here there was a healthy state of being which put us to shame. There was also another kind of 'knowledge' by which tom-tom and dance violently portrayed the intimacy we are quite unaware of between man and the cosmos. . . .

I think that a black dancer who improvises his rhythms beneath the palm leaves shining like blades in the moonlight, is more master of the cosmos and impresses me more than an astronaut sent to the moon.

I don't want to be misunderstood. Like everyone else I felt proud to be a man when I saw on television the first man walking on the moon. I mean simply that the rocket is 'alien' to the spaces through which it travels. It challenges them. The astronauts were able to tell us what they found on the moon. I think an African could teach us 'who the moon is'.

The black dancer who attracts all eyes and whose inspiration releases the delirious beating of the tom-tom, is a cosmic figure. He is Man. Total Man.

I felt ill at ease. My Church had transplanted into this exotic setting the gentle groans of its harmoniums, the whole pious paraphernalia of Saint Sulpice, and the Ewondo language which lives on rhythms, and is music, was violated by the little tunes of the ancient songs of my childhood. . . .

The black Christians sang Gregorian chant in Latin. They sang very well. . . . And Gregorian chant is so beautiful. . . .

But why was my Church, whose vocation was to be offered to life, all forms of life, to celebrate and offer up every side of man, why, with all its treasures of love, was it so slow to understand that love's tenderness is also to 'welcome'?

However, my Church had taught me that the sweetest joy you can offer a poor man is to accept his humble gift: when a poor man also has the chance to give, he acquires human dignity.

But there was a misunderstanding: in Africa I had not come among the poor. They were rich. Immensely rich.

But because the West does not recognize any culture other than its own, or other standards or other gods, it has despised and ignored the African genius, without realizing that it contained new sources of life completely lacking in western culture.

God was made MAN . . . we are told. The Church had turned this into 'God became western man'.

Perhaps I may be accused of injustice and of forgetting all that the Church and the West – alas, the two are dangerously synonymous here – have given to the black people. I know: hospitals, dispensaries, schools, roads, railways, technology . . . then money, wine, alcohol. . . . But I do not dispute this. Even if all these gifts were not totally single-minded, I don't want to go into this question, even though it is a serious one. What worries me is: 'What have we received from Africa?' 'What has changed in the West since it has come to know Africa?' Apart from exotic consumer goods. This is where the injustice begins.

Europe crushed us flat
beneath its tanks' pachydermatous feet.
We cried out our pain in the night.
There was no one to answer our cry.
The Church's princes had nothing to say;
politicians howled hyena generosity.
But black people matter.
People matter.
No they don't, when Europe matters more.
   (Senghor, *Black Hosts*)

What 'man' did colonization and the missionaries want to meet in Africa? The 'man' whose definition they had worked out over the centuries. Western man was the pattern, the archetype; his culture, morality, and rites were the measure of life. The African genius was not foreseen in the construction of their world. However, the African bush is rich soil for poetry. There is mystery in the bright quivering light, the murmur of insects, the velvety cries of the great blue birds, the calm swaying of the top-heavy palm trees and the vibration of the forest under the burning sky, all the luxuriant greenery and the sweet scent of the ilang-ilang, the nightmare whorls of the great creepers, and the perfection of the silvery branches which suddenly emerge from this profusion and stand out pure against the sky . . . this is Africa, and this treasure, the mystery of the forest, quivering and pulsing, is the African's home: he stands out in the harmony of his forest like the soloist in a concerto composed by the cosmos.

He has something to tell us.

I have seen bush women praying. They improvised real psalms with syncopated verses, whose refrain was taken up full voiced by the crowd.

This was in the magnificent cathedral of the forest, by torchlight, to the rhythm of batons pounding the earth. I stopped, my teeth were clenched with emotion, and I was filled with joy because a people was freeing its own particular genius to pray its own prayer.

Our dances are our gift to you.
Listen to our batons beating the earth.
This is our prayer.
And the intoxicating tom-tom
is our prayer to you.

The trail leading the black people to the source is a winding one. But they found it for themselves. This trail takes irrational turnings – irrational to us shameless Cartesians – but it leads through the forest to the source. The trail 'belongs' to the forest.

This is what African logic is like. It is an immediate intuition of the present moment. You must go on seizing each moment as it passes, from sensation to sensation, and 'knowledge' is 'communion' with all life's intoxicating pulses. . . . So they dance. . . .

A few miles from here a village is dancing under the stars. The tom-tom beats out its rhythm, 1-2-3, 1-2, 1-2-3, 1-2 and the cries of the dancers echo through the forest. They are carried to me on the soft night breeze. They die down and then burst out again, like the breath of night: crickets and strange insects vibrate.

There are two tom-toms. The first is muffled and intoxicating, the other is dry and breathless. Sometimes it breaks up the first tom-tom's rhythm with a series of rapid beats.

It is obsessive but beautiful.

It is life, the life of a people.

The West has been invited to the party. It could become intoxicated by these fresh experiences. And we would have seen the African smile broadly at our petty certainties. But the West has nothing to learn. The West is a 'result'. Africa was an intoxication offered to us. We spurned it. Spurning is killing.

I had a long conversation with an old leper woman. We were both sitting on the ground. I found it restful to do nothing but echo her voice. She was muttering to herself . . . and I could only just catch the words issuing from her toothless mouth. She was old and what she expressed in her mumbling was a certain security and simple peace. . . .

I was sitting on the ground, resting on one hand and with my legs tucked under me. I became lost in her incoherent monologue reflecting a life which for decades had been bounded by this lost village with its familiar chickens and leaping goats. There was only this old woman, ravaged by leprosy, with nearly a century's history in her little witchlike eyes. I just let her talk and 'be'. With her I felt a primitive awareness in myself of a strong and painful bond to life. Life, her only treasure. She taught me self-awareness by my receptivity. I felt it was pure poetry, poetry as a state regained, near to the simple source.

And I tell you, western world and you, France, my own beautiful country, that in Africa there was a people for us to meet, not to conquer. They could have taught you their language, and what goes beyond words, their deep pulse of life. And the awareness given us by true meeting is richer and more authentic than any book. I had to accept being, 'being with Africa'. With all the horizons it offered to mankind as a whole. The West would not have denied its own culture, but enriched and ennobled it.

This was a new country, a new range of awareness, which should not have been measured by western standards. The black people were not a 'phenomenon' to be judged by comparison. What was wanted was not adaptation but being. And growing together.

In a tiny village quite hidden in the bush, yesterday evening a great thunderbolt crashed across the sky. Then the wind rose and a long groan passed through the trees. There was a state of alert. The master of the house warned me before I went to bed: 'If the tornado comes . . .' with detailed instructions of what I should do: take books, papers, table, chairs to places where the water usually did not reach. I took care to store my treasures in my trunk. The great wind rose and the whole forest shuddered in pain. The little hut was attacked by the hosts of heaven and the storm-winds beat upon it like great waves. The sky roared: not with the far-off roar announcing the coming of the storm, but implacably present. The great monster circled the sky above the sleeping village and the crazed palm trees. The first drops fell on the dried-out rushes. Then the storm broke and there was another clap of thunder. It was one of the worst tornadoes I had ever experienced.

I did not resist. I opened the fragile door and the wind battered me. The rain beat down upon the land which was transformed by the blue lightning flashes. There were great explosions followed by rumbles. There were moments of silence when the wind and the rain beat down. Moments of silence in which the tension built up to explode again in another violent thunderbolt.

I went inside. The peace of my little hut made me smile. I went back to my campbed, thinking of the black people huddled like me, tonight, under their roofs of rushes. I thought of all the black children, in their little bamboo beds, who were so sound asleep that very few of them would mention the storm tomorrow.

I thought of the people of God who recognized the voice of the Lord in the thunder 3000 years ago.

I thought of the black people, who only a hundred years ago had as their only refuge their roofs of rushes and their incantations. The black people are battered six months out of twelve by storms. And I remembered a little schoolboy walking through the storm, whose only protection had been a banana leaf he had picked on the wayside. He was careless and re-signed. . . . 'Resigned'. A battered people. By the forest, by the sun, by tornadoes. A resigned people.

And the black child who walked through the rain, sodden and uncaring, seemed more connected to the cosmos by his resignation than by the banana leaf which the wind tore from his head.

Thereafter the black people became resigned in other – tragic – ways. But neither their incantations nor their dancing could deliver them from the infernal tornado that hit them when they met the West.

The first contact this proud people had with mine was the slave trade, which over several decades tore from Africa tens of millions of her finest sons.

We must see and understand.

Black and White

My experience in Africa was brought to an end – alas – by the unexpected failure of my health. It's well known that animals are far less dangerous than microbes.

I was in the heart of the bush, curate to an African priest. Not his technical adviser, but his curate, his deputy, delivered over to his way of looking at men and life, to bear with him the weight of his people, to learn and learn again, each of us offering the other the best of himself, to indicate, far beyond ourselves, that every proclamation of the gospel is exchange and dialogue, that all love is presence and sharing.

I have already said that in creating man in his own image God was expressing himself. And with such richness that when God wants to speak to man he uses man as the alphabet.

We must therefore drink deep from all the springs from which any human greatness wells, get to know the whole alphabet of flesh and blood scattered across the world, in order to read Jesus Christ, who is present everywhere.

I liked my black parish priest, and he liked me. And it was good to be so different in the evening, in the stridency of the night, when the flame of the storm-lamp flickered between us like a butterfly's wing and we had nothing to give each other in the semi-darkness except our eyes. He was black and I was white. We were free. Each of us took up the burden of his origins and his destiny, and the reciprocal going-out beyond ourselves slowly gave birth to communion.

Sometimes we recognized together the secret movements of the heart, the body, the mind, when they rose from the great deeps to reveal to us the common sources and the universal man which each of us bears within himself.

Sometimes we would let ourselves be carried along, down there, a long way, far beyond ourselves, towards the face we recognized together, the face of Jesus.

And in those exchanges, in which the words counted for less than the silences, I, the white man, began to discover, in the face of my black parish priest, the other face of the Church. And it was there, in that encounter, more than anywhere else, that I grew in the faith.

Sometimes, too, I would grow grave, and, as I pondered my certainties and my metaphysical problems, suddenly a mighty burst of laughter – the great negro laugh – would drown my internal debates in a flash.

He used to laugh. He had a good laugh, my black parish priest. It was healthy laughter. It was his intelligence laughing. And that laugh is contagious.

Then we would together plumb the depths of those moments in which thought, trying to be pure, found itself even purer for merging with the joy of existing, that other form of truth to self.

Yes, we were free. And freedom saved both of us from that dangerous word adaptation. I learned to be suspicious of that word. It has sometimes been made the key word, the magic word, the word which unlocks all human contacts. In spite of that it is the admission of a betrayal: to adapt is to recognize the phenomenon of foreignness. It sets the seal on distances. Adapting makes it hard to avoid artificiality. I can scarcely think of any creatures except angels or monsters who would need to adapt to man.

Either one is a man among men – white, black, yellow, red, Jew, Arab – perhaps a prisoner of the 'bag of skin' which limits every human person, but a man who eats, drinks, sings, cries, suffers, and dies. Let there be no more talk of adaptation.

Or one is a monster, condemned to solitude, a special case (in Greek *idios* – idiot!), and maladjusted for ever.

One adapts to human techniques and the social climates they bring. One doesn't adapt to men, on pain of renouncing one's status as a man.

Jesus said:

'We played the pipes for you, and you wouldn't dance.' (Luke 7.32, JB)

Dancing is what is wanted, not smiles at the dancers.

'We sang dirges and you wouldn't cry.'   (Luke 7.32, JB)

Tears are wanted, not exhortations to the tearful.

My life in Africa taught me to prefer 'burial' to adaptation. Adaptation offers sympathy. Burial is 'empathy'. Perhaps this is the deepest culture, 'capacity' for the other, 'passibility' for the other. This culture is what I learned from a black priest.

He was my parish priest. He was my boss.

He is my friend. My brother.

I remember his welcome. I remember the 'shared existence' we attempted together. I remember his face at the hospital when we made our farewells. A beautiful black face, wet with tears. I have kept that face in me. And I can dream of unity. I am not saying that everything was easy. It takes time, a lot of time, to create unity. People often forget the importance of time for getting to know each other. Free time, wasted time. Beings do not meet simply through the agreement of their speech, their dreams, their ideas. And even if, in the early stages, stirred emotions can create the illusion of unity, it only takes a little lucidity to know that trust in the passing of time is still needed. Time slowly secretes, unknown to us, the imponderables of reciprocal knowledge. Time buries us in itself and shapes us gently one for the other. I know hundreds of dramas of love in which people separate because they haven't taken the time to wait for each other.

It is not the work done together which does most to forge 'the common being', but the time spent together.

On this point Africa is a good school, perhaps because it has been able to keep firm ties with the earth and the cosmos when we have lost them. It knows the patience with which its great trees grow.

We are horrified spectators of the passing of time. The implacable rhythm of the pendulum dispatches each of our precious seconds, the second-hand of our watch rushes on, nibbling steadily, and finally the macabre voice of the speaking clock talks to us about the passing of time like the executioner talking to his victim. They have all turned us into slaves of time. Time has become money, the worst of tyrants. It has become the road which takes us to death.

In Africa time is time for living.

So I admit that it wasn't easy, when I agreed to share the life of an African priest, to give up abruptly the action, the organization of time, the 'race against the clock', the fever to get things done fast in exchange for this apparent stagnation in which I learned that things 'do themselves' even when you don't do them frenetically. The 'passing of time' is not 'a waste of time' if the time is charged with presence.

And my black parish priest's attitude to his people, his

country, and his life, even if it irritated my impatience for action, showed me that the sovereign serenity which lets itself be carried along by time is also, finally, very effective, and less dangerous than the fever and anguish which fight 'against' time.

In the bush there are no nervous breakdowns. They have nothing but the sun to tell them it's noon. What a fortunate people who still have to look at the sun to live. We have lost the sun's complicity. We have no time left.

As I say, it wasn't easy to live with my black parish priest by these rhythms which were so new to me. My whole western formation – my deformation – resisted it. The idea of time brings with it into everyday life attitudes, reactions to events, and a psychological life which, in their turn, modify the work-ings of thought, the logic or arguments, the priorities of the attention and, of course, the very life of language, the meaning of dialogue and exchange.

It wasn't easy, but I want to say how surprised I am at the reaction of my European friends when I describe these mem-ories. People always admire my patience, my self-denial. They never tell me about the patience and self-denial of my black parish priest. It's so obvious that we here in the West possess the truth about man and life. But in fact the life I shared with an African had nothing at all to do with patience and self-denial. You need patience when you pretend. When you're really living, you're led on by the fascination, and the very difficulty, which every day reveals new potential for life to be tapped, merges with the passion to become.

The only patience I needed – and I'm sure my African friend needed it more often than me – was with myself, with the idiotic impatience of my breathless western deformities. Between my black parish priest and me, the debt is on my side.

Since then I have met many men pursued by themselves, fragments of loves, ruins of dreams, so many neuroses, so many psychoses, because people hadn't taken the 'time to live'.

Africa can still teach us that too.

And Now?

We may well feel pity for the fate of Africa and the Third World. We may well feel embarrassment and guilt at belonging to social structures which tolerate the existence of the hungry world. We may even be beginning to feel fear at the gusts of revolutionary violence from the poor peoples, the vast planetary proletariat which is today rising to demand its dues. We may well undergo a radical change of attitude to the 'exploited' of yesterday when they, suddenly realizing the enormous power of their oil, deliberately tilt the world economy for their sole benefit. See the exploiter exploited. See the West on its knees.

And what does that change? Nothing.

I am not an economist. I am not a sociologist. I am only a priest of the Church of Jesus Christ. In that capacity I have pursued men and their mystery; again in that capacity I was able to live the finest years of my life in Africa.

Even if my Church, in the course of its history, has been able to alienate, or let itself be alienated by political or social structures which have sometimes deformed it, I know all the potential for liberation it bears in itself.

My only subject in writing this book is man and that powerful movement, profound and invincible, which he never ceases to reveal even in his weariness and in his revolts – especially in his revolts – towards transcendence, towards that creator God whose breath he breathes even if he doesn't give him a name, even if he doesn't give him his name.

I believe in God, I believe in man, and even if the value of my evidence runs the risk of being reduced because it rejects the sombre prestige of violence or the facile glitter of partisan policies, I do not want any other support than my faith in God, my faith in man. They are the same, since for me, as I have said, man is relation to God.

If all believers rediscovered the sense of that dimension, not as 'ideology', but in real life, we could at last begin to talk about liberation, reconciliation, unity. We could at last start making the revolution.

Are not the carefully planned, fragmentary revolutions which take place in fury and blood, and the great wrath of the poor which we hear rumbling all over the world, are they not simply the cry of humanity which comes from beyond the ages, and which reveals in rage and despair the finest roots of man, who was created to live free and to love?

And in all this outcry I still want to see the divine dimension. When a man proclaims his misfortune, it is always God calling.

No one, believer or unbeliever, can deny my claim that all man is in every man, all man is in all men, and that we are witnessing today, among so many disasters, the appearance of new fervours, new utopias, irreversible dynamisms, all converging on what one cannot call by any other name than the Absolute.

Here believers and unbelievers meet.

Let's not talk about the indifferent. They aren't involved. They have no right to speak. Why should they have? There is a greatness in the faith, there is a greatness in unbelief. Indifference is an admission of a lack of solidity. It is in brackets, has not yet reached the threshold of freedom. The indifferent person has not 'chosen' himself. Is there such a person? And if people who are indifferent get irritated when they read these lines, then they aren't indifferent.

Help for the Third World, from now on, is the salvation of the West. The future of the 'total man' depends on it.

> What the Third World expects from those who have kept it in slavery for centuries, writes Frantz Fanon, is that they should help to rehabilitate man, to ensure the triumph of man everywhere, once and for all. . . .

> For Europe, for ourselves and for humanity, comrades, we must turn over a new leaf, we must work out new concepts, and try to set afoot a new man.[1]

This is the moment to reread the letter attributed to the apostle James:

> Now an answer for the rich. Start crying, weep. . . . Your wealth is all rotting. . . . Labourers mowed your fields, and you cheated them . . . in the time of slaughter you went on eating to your heart's content. It was you who condemned

85

the innocent and killed them; they offered you no resistance. (Jas. 5.1–2, 4–6, JB)

It is a provocative and disturbing text. If, instead of being taken from the Bible and signed by the man who was called 'the brother of the Lord', if, instead of being 'inspired' by the breath of God, those words came from a modern preacher, or were in a statement from one of our bishops, it is quite likely, alas, that they would scandalize quite a number of pious people.

We could perhaps understand such passionate, violent, revolutionary language from the pen of Paul or John. But they were written by James, the first bishop of Jerusalem, whose reputation for wisdom was established throughout the infant Church, and who, on several occasions, set his attitude of serenity and firmness against Paul's apostolic impulsiveness.

His letter is permeated by the Bible. It gathers together the inspiration and fervour of the greatest of the prophets and, even in its language, the whole tension of the message of Jesus and the beatitudes.

It is therefore out of the question, unless we are to be dishonest, to defuse the violence of this text or limit its application on the pretext that this letter was written in the fifties of our era and that times have changed. Unfortunately, times haven't changed. When it was the apostles who were proclaiming the gospel, encyclicals sounded like that. And yet the problem of poverty to which the apostle James refers was very local. But in those days the gospel made demands. It was an urgent task, the creation of man, a new man.

Today the problem of the poor is worldwide. And the terrifying distortion which divides the world of the poor and the world of the rich lays us all, perhaps personally, but collectively quite certainly, open to the charges in that letter.

This is God's view of what we are doing with life and the human world, and James is the prophet charged with conveying it to us. Like all the great prophets, he is overwhelmed by the sovereign presence of God to man, overwhelmed by the distress of the poor. So he speaks, and his message is a cry which rebounds down the length of history until it reaches our consciences today.

In Africa I tried my best to share the life of the poor. Today it is my only real wealth. I encountered, like a nightmare, the hideous face of the leper. I saw that 'slow entry of death into life' (Péguy) which is called poverty. I was an impotent witness of the despair of these men imprisoned in their black skins, for whom the five words 'I am a black man' had become five bars enclosing an immense loneliness, outside which, perhaps, it would have been possible to live.

The Third World. It is we, the well-fed, who gave it the horrible name which is a condemnation of ourselves: 'The hungry world.'

We need to have measured the immense expectation of those eyes fixed on us. We need to have measured the terrible silence of those hundreds of millions of starving men, women, and children, skeletons clinging to a fragile life, and that tragic look which eats away their faces.

We need to stop for a moment the insane pace of our lives, stuffed as they are with wealth, in order to hear finally the din of war, the long silence of the oppressed, the cries of hate, and the silence, the awful silence of death, when the executioners have won.

Then we can understand the apostle James's terrible letter. It is addressed to us. The rich country is us. That western world we are so proud of, where all the riches of the earth pile up, is us. Money, comfort, luxury surround us, and the West controls all the laws of the world market.

And what is this civilization where it becomes possible, reasonable, and even wise to justify bombs and squander fabulous sums in the service of massacre and death?

> Now an answer for the rich. Start crying, weep for the miseries that are coming to you. Your wealth is all rotting, your clothes are all eaten up by moths. All your gold and your silver are corroding away . . . you have had a life of comfort and luxury; in the time of slaughter you went on eating to your heart's content. It was you who condemned the innocent and killed them; they offered you no resistance. (Jas. 5.1–3, 5–6, JB)

Let no one say – oh, no – let no one say, 'I can't do anything about it', that these are all world problems, problems of economics, politics, and finance, and that only people with universal powers could solve them.

87

And we hear every day about the great powers of this world. The three powers, the four powers, and even the superpowers. But as far as I am concerned, I don't want to hear about any more than two great powers on earth. The first is poverty. The second is love.

It is there, in the confrontation between these two great giants, that the destiny of man is decided. And it is there that Jesus took his place among us. And, whether we like it or not, for 2000 years that has been the place of all Christians.

After all, those whom we call, without smiling, the powerful people of this world, were put on their thrones by us, and the public opinion they keep on polling, which so often shapes them, is us too: we find ourselves dreaming of freedom.

For if all the free men on earth, all the men of good will, all Christians suddenly began to speak out in their turn and echo the letter of the apostle James, and denounce injustice and tear aside hypocrisy, then we would see the first rays of hope for the poor dawn on our earth.

'I was hungry and you gave me food,' says Jesus. The poverty and distress of the world, without the support of love, is a massacre. Without love egoisms harden, men revolt, and all the great furies break free and rule the world: and war and hatred and sex and death.

Or love can take responsibility for the suffering and wretchedness of the world, and then peace and joy come down to earth.

And there is charity.

The only sign Jesus sent John the Baptist in prison to prove that he was the Messiah was this:

'Go and tell John that the poor have the good news preached to them.'

Perhaps it would be enough for each of us to summon up the enormous power of his or her own tenderness, look at the world and life with the eyes of our God, a God who loves, a God who saves, and stand up among our brothers and sisters and shout out each in turn the letter of James, the 'good news', the 'gospel'. That might finally give all those who fall, all those who are going to die, the right to live free and the happiness of loving.

Come, O blessed of my Father. . . .
for I was hungry and you gave me food,
I was thirsty and you gave me drink,
I was a stranger and you welcomed me,
I was naked and you clothed me,
I was sick and you visited me,
I was in prison and you came to me.   (Matt. 25.34–6)

That is what God is like.
That is what man is like.
That is what the revolution is like.

When Jesus said, 'You have heard that it was said . . . but I say to you . . .' he was not very far from revolutionary language. So close, in fact, that he died for it.

Often the revolutionary bears within him currents which submerge him. His shouts on the barricades come from further away than himself and go further than him. He is a consciousness receiving an impulse of history, a straining for growth. The revolutionary cry is the explosion of a consciousness invaded by the brutal demand of man's destiny. At this point of truth, at this point of clarity, at this point of no return, when it is necessary to shout, to scream and, sometimes, to break things.

One could read all the prophets of the Bible and find the same feeling.

A Christian is constantly questioning the value of his actions – it is his vocation. Every injustice, every case of suffering, every form of oppression does violence to him and challenges him. Because of this the Christian is a danger to structures and the established order. That is, if Constantine is really dead. And if Jesus is really alive.

Jesus is a question facing man. The gospel is a task to be carried out. Because God's creation is unfinished and is from now on in man's hands.

And now, what is to be done?

First of all we must for ever strike out of our vocabulary the horrible words which divide us, 'Third World' or, even, worse, 'hungry world'. There are human beings. There are human faces. There is 'the world'. And if the poorest peoples really need a name, let's be brave: they are 'the world of shame' because they are poor and hungry *because of us*. This is the 'sin of the world' today. And the Church's vocation for 2000 years has been to face the sin of the world and try to reduce it.

The whole of the Church's missionary adventure today is here. One doesn't become a missionary by crossing the sea and leaving one's family, one's country, one's wealth, and one's culture to go to distant shores. One is a missionary because one is baptized and involved in a Christian community in the world's struggle.

One doesn't choose to be or not to be a missionary as though it were an optional virtue which could be added depending on whether one was more or less generous, more or less concerned. One is a missionary because one is baptized, a child of God, and, by virtue of that, absorbed by the call of the poor, by the tension of the Church of Jesus to provide everywhere the radiant presence of a hope and to proclaim the whole dimension of man and of his destiny by bearing witness to the gospel.

Baptism is a call to us to be missionaries. Baptism qualifies us to be missionaries. Baptism appoints us missionaries.

There are those who perform gestures and there are those who perform actions. This is a good example of a Sartrean language which is ideally suited to the Christians of our time, faced with the world 'of shame'. 'Gestures', even very generous ones, money, almsgiving, release us from obligation – simple. 'Actions', even very humble ones, are dangerous – there's no going back.

I'm well aware that the history of the missions has hardly made us used to this language. It remains true that, to many Christians, missionary work, linked as it was from the start with the great colonial adventures, still means basically the 'export' of the faith and its rites and morality as practised in the West.

So, in the past, the ships of Spain (and other countries) landed together on the distant shores both the colonial army and the missionary clergy, and it became the custom through the centuries to plant simultaneously the flag and the cross. This is not the place to analyse the glories and the misdeeds of those bygone days: we know well that they produced famous heroes and martyrs. We also know that not everything was pure. And what we forget in particular is that those countries colonized in the past are still suffering from our deeds of valour.

It's true that I met in Africa genuine pioneers: bishops, priests, men and women religious, laypeople, believers, unbelievers, whose glorious past and tireless generosity compel respect, even if the missionary strategy of their time is now unthinkable. Heroes are only right at one time.

After the war, as a new world began to grow, the Church acquired a new awareness. Missionary work now finally stopped being that 'export' of the western Christian faith which, as I can testify, has so often collided with, and sometimes condemned, the genius of a people, its unique customs, and the very sense of the sacred which inspired them. It became a meeting, dialogue, and sharing in which the awakening of minds, respect for the mystery of the person, and the development of liberties make it possible to grow together.

I discovered this at the Council, one of the most beautiful experiences of the universal Church, where the bishops of the whole world revealed to all nations that they were first of all listening to each other. At the Council I met bishops from all corners of the poor world: Dom Helder Camara, that great prophet of our time, and with him the anguish and distress of Brazil; Mgr Laraïn, a bishop from Chile, who talked to us with serenity about his people's hope, and died before the great disaster we witnessed; Mgr Nagae, the bishop of Tokyo, who used to say to us, 'You western Christians, you talk about "planting" the Church among other peoples as though you first had to grow the seed in your countries. . . . Jesus said, "The sower goes out to sow. . . . He trusts the soil." ' And Mgr Zoa, who became my bishop in Yaounde after ten years of shared work and deep friendship, who kept saying to me, 'Let them leave us alone, leave us to realize who we are.'

I would like to mention them all here, the Asians, the Africans, the South Americans, and express our amazement and, sometimes, our confusion in the face of these young Christianities which were suddenly showing us 'the other face' of the Church, 'the other face' of Jesus, the one they had shaped as lovingly and as generously as we.

And, confronted with this other face of the faith, which was coming to us from poverty, distress, and hunger, we had – at last – everything to learn. We now found that the chief missionary virtue is not so much to be a teacher as to be teachable, and that the missionary who crosses the sea is going out to meet the Spirit, to draw on his presence hidden under other forms of the sacred and of human nature.

This is perhaps the main mission of the Church, of Christians, to the world of the poor; a certain way of looking.

Our attitudes are tired, worn, blunted. They have become automatic. We are settled in the security of our familiar surroundings, our structures, our standards, and our attitudes are attitudes of judgement.

We need new perceptions, perceptions freed from the past, stimulated by the future. Perceptions new every morning, perceptions capable of astonishment, still capable of learning. Perceptions on the alert. We need an attitude which doesn't ask questions or impose conditions, an attitude which is already an intuitive awareness of possibilities. A creative attitude, God's attitude to man.

I think of the miracle of the multiplication of the loaves. There is a starving crowd, out in the desert (Mark 6.30–44). The apostles' attitude: 'Send the crowd away. . . .' Just our attitude, our solution, to the problem of immigrants. Jesus's attitude: 'I'm sorry for that crowd.' And immediate action. Not an easy miracle. Jesus sends his team of apostles into action. 'You give them something to eat.' They say to him, 'It's impossible.' He retorts, 'How many loaves have you got? Go and see.' That is man. I admit that the wonder of the miracle which follows is of only secondary interest to me. I am concentrating on what seems to me here the essential.

If we start from a certain way of looking at distress, even if the effort is beyond our strength, all 'miracles' are possible. We need the eyes of faith, faith in man, faith in God. Then you can feed 5000 people with five loaves and two fishes.

The whole history of the relation of man to God, of God to man, in other words, the whole of the Bible, the whole meaning of the incarnation, the story of a God 'made man', the whole history of the Church from the beginning to our own time, all comes down to this: God's attitude to me, forcing me to take up an attitude to man, the world, and life.

When his faithful people boast of their prayers, fasts, and sacrifices, God sends them away, sometimes violently, to the poor, 'the stranger, the widow, the orphan in the midst of you'.

Jesus said, 'I am sending you out. . . . You give them something to eat. . . . I will make you fishers of men. . . .', etc.

The Christian is, by definition, the 'bridge' between man and God (pontiff, *pontifex*, 'bridgebuilder'), between God and man. To complete creation. Leaving out either of the terms is denying that one is a child of God.

Some people are so afraid of losing God that they forget man. Others are so afraid of losing man that they forget God.

I recognize that one kind of Christian education used to give very little preparation for this sort of attitude. We had learned to concentrate on our own salvation. The world was the business of a sovereign God, not ours. And often we believed in order to avoid the effort to understand. Before God we pleaded, begged, and appealed. There was heaven and there was hell. We soon confused faith and morality, prayer and devotion, charity and almsgiving, the practice of the sacraments and the sacramental life.

We kept away from action to preserve contemplation, we kept away from politics to protect religion, we kept away from earth to safeguard heaven, we kept away from man to reassure God.

'You give them something to eat.' In the face of the enormity of the scandal, and if we want to be honest with ourselves, it is now clear that it is laughable to talk about 'reconciliation' without first engaging in – with all the boldness which such an enterprise requires – a *political* analysis of the causes which have created the inhuman separation between us and the poor. When structures are a scandal, the Christian becomes dangerous for the structures.

Political analysis, political information, taking a political position, political commitment and struggle, are a Christian duty.

I do mean 'political'. But we mustn't reduce the word to the level of partisan ideology and propaganda, whether from the right, the centre, or the left. And we have to face the fact that our big political parties, which are so often prisoners of their own strategy, have all, or almost all, settled for evading, if not ignoring, the scandal of the poor world.

'Political' means that profound movement made up of the nobility of intelligence and generosity because it raises our eyes from our petty calculations, our securities, our profits, our interests, and mobilizes us totally in the service of man and of his destiny.

Political commitment is connected with man's relation to God. It shares in that powerful movement which every man bears in him to draw mankind and the whole universe towards the completion of creation. It is a duty of faith.

It is impossible to be a Christian and neutral without betraying God's attitude to the world.

'You give them something to eat. . . . How many loaves have you got? Go and see.'

NOTE

1   Frantz Fanon, *The Wretched of the Earth*. London, 1965, p. 255.

Job Today

The Bible contains an amazing book, the Book of Job.

I am not here offering an exegesis of Job. I just want to discuss it like a modern book. For, apart from the style and the setting of this extraordinary poem, all the ravings and cries of Job as he is torn between his pain and his faith in a just and good God are our own. I have heard them – and uttered them myself – too often not to try to echo them here.

In the Book of Job we also find the exasperating chatter of the 'comforters', full of principles, doctrines, beliefs, and nonsense. . . . They are unfamiliar with silence because their silence is empty and it frightens them. They are unfamiliar with suffering because suffering is one of the few things which, in the depths of loneliness into which it plunges us, reveals to us that ocean of silence so close to the silence of death, where great encounters take place.

We have to read the Book of Job and pay attention to all the silences. Listen to Job in simultaneous wonder and horror. Listen to the complaints and blasphemies of Job, 'the man', and beg him to be quiet and beg him to go on shouting. Now we are torn between the freedom which wants to know the extent of the misfortune and the agony of experiencing it. And we remember that we are men, men of flesh and blood, and that Job's long, passionate complaint is also, every day, the clamour of the world.

> Let the day perish wherein I was born,
> and the night which said,
> 'A man-child is conceived.'
> Let that day be darkness! . . .
> Let gloom and deep darkness claim it. . . .
> Let that night be barren;
> Let no joyful cry be heard in it.
> Let those curse it who curse the day. . . .
> Let the stars of its dawn be dark;
> let it hope for light, but have none,
> nor see the eyelids of the morning;

because it did not shut the doors of my mother's womb,
nor hide trouble from my eyes.
Why did I not die at birth? . . .
Why did the knees receive me?
Or why the breasts, that I should suck?
Why is light given to him that is in misery? . . .
(Job 3.3–5, 7–12, 20)

Job is despair.

He is the shattered man who came to see me. He had destroyed his child, his own son, with a destruction more terrible than death.

He is the young woman on drugs who showed me her revolver in her frail hand and softly murmured words of farewell. Her features, frozen by an excess of pain, seemed already turned towards other shores. A revolver anyway is not only frightening, it is also hideous with all the ugliness of the world, and the delicate fingers of a woman's hand tightening on its handle are suddenly a diabolic force.

He is the face of a young girl whose eyes could no longer even weep: two youths had dragged her off and raped her in a car.

He is the insane man who went before my eyes from lucidity to raving, thrashing in an incoherent argument in an attempt to hang on to reality, and sinking into his darkness like a drowning man into the grey, cold water. Despair was the moment when his eyes saw me again.

No wonder then if I cannot keep silence;
in the anguish of my spirit I must speak,
lament in the bitterness of my soul.
Strangling I would welcome rather,
and death itself, than these my sufferings.
I waste away, my life is not unending;
leave me then, for my days are but a breath.
What is man that you should make so much of him,
subjecting him to your scrutiny,
that morning after morning you should examine him
and at every instant test him?
Will you never take your eyes off me
long enough for me to swallow my spittle?

Suppose I have sinned, what have I done to you,
　　you tireless watcher of mankind?
Why do you choose me as your target?
　　(Job 7.11, 15–20, JB)

Despair. I could now write a book about these furthest limits of distress.

But there is the Book of Job. It is inspired by the Spirit. It is the book of sovereign freedom, in which a man on his own, with his failed life in his hands, dominates the chattering of his comforters with the weight of his despair.

They are always there, the learned ones, the casuists, the moralists, the analysts, the ghouls. They are there with their traditions, with their convictions, with their distinctions, their interpretations, with all their learning, their categories, and their well-filled card indexes.

They know. It's their job to know. They're dried up with knowing. Their obsession is the answer which has to be found. They can't imagine a problem without an answer because they've filed God among their moral categories. They are there round Job. And if Job is stubborn, they are teachers and so they are right.

Yes, they are always there. With 'reasons'. They don't know. The satisfied don't know. There's no hope of their knowing that suffering can't be explained, and that between the rigour of the law and its application there is always the human person.

They think they know misery. All they have is knowledge. And you need experience.

Job has answered all these vile comforters once and for all. The world is full of them, pharisees, hypocrites, good people.

Job has given an answer once and for all to all the detestable comforters the world is so full of, to all the pharisees, all the hypocrites, all the people with the right views, those professional blunderers who provoke the revolt of the poor and whom misery laughs to scorn.

　　. . . miserable comforters are you all.
　　Shall windy words have an end?
　　　　Or what provokes you that you answer?
　　I also could speak as you do,
　　　　if you were in my place;
　　I could join words together against you,
　　　　and shake my head at you.　(Job 16.2–4)

What you know, I also know;
    I am not inferior to you.
But I would speak to the Almighty,
    and I desire to argue my case with God.
As for you, you whitewash with lies;
    worthless physicians are you all.
Oh that you would keep silent,
    and it would be your wisdom!
Will you speak falsely for God,
    and speak deceitfully for him? . . .
Or can you deceive him, as one deceives a man? . . .
Your maxims are proverbs of ashes,
    your defences are defences of clay.
Let me have silence, and I will speak. . . .
    (Job 13.2–5, 7, 9, 12–13)

The Bible is the word of God. It is moving, when we read the Book of Job, to think that these great human cries are inspired by the breath of the Spirit just as much as the most serene contemplations. Here God gets involved. He merges with distress.

Notice that Job doesn't appeal to God. He doesn't plead with him. He confronts God, challenges him, and brings him before the court of misery.

And God listens. He will speak in his turn. The Book of Job ends with God's defence.

This is an aspect of the relation of man to God which is too often neglected. One way that relation can be expressed is in the sudden revolt of those whom life oppresses, who have nothing left to defend but their freedom.

Backs to the wall and with bare hands, alone, defeated, but still on their feet. They have worn out adversity. They have no tears left. Even their deaths are useless. They are the ones who have lost everything, who have gained nothing. They have been betrayed by life, betrayed by love. Dispossessed, naked, but supremely free.

God himself, the God to whom they had given everything, God himself has betrayed them.

In this situation faith is confronted by the invincible power of freedom.

... every fibre of my heart is broken.
Night, they say, makes room for day,
    and light is near at hand to chase the darkness.
All I look forward to is dwelling in Sheol,
    and making my bed in the dark.
I tell the tomb, 'You are my father',
    and call the worm my mother and my sister.
Where then is my hope?
    Who can see any happiness for me?
    (Job 17.11–15, JB)

... God, you must know, is my oppressor,
    and his is the net that closes round me.
If I protest against such violence, there is no reply;
    if I appeal against it, judgement is never given.
He has built a wall across my path which I cannot pass,
    and covered my way with darkness.
He has stolen my honour away. . . .
As a man a shrub, so he uproots my hope.
    (Job 19.6–10, JB)

God is no longer there to turn to. He is no longer a power. Faithfulness to oneself confronts faithfulness to God. It is a marvellous argument in which freedom, disdaining the derisory language of men, their laws, and their traditions, stands up straight and raises itself to face God in an encounter in which all risks are possible because they are dictated by the nobility of being a man.

There should be no talk of pride here. That is what the advisers round Job say. Pride creeps along the ground and puts its roots into the thickness of the self. Pride is enjoyment of self.

Job is freedom. Freedom is pure.

Kierkegaard, the great philosopher poet, who lived in his flesh all the torments of the absurd, Kierkegaard turned to Job:

Speak, unforgettable Job! Repeat all your words, powerful advocate appearing before the tribunal of the Most High with the fearlessness of a roaring lion.

Your words reveal the force, and your heart reveals the fear, of God. Even when you groan, when you protect your despair against your friends ready to attack you with their speeches, even when you lose patience with their arguments

99

and reduce their wisdom to dust and pour scorn on their defences of God, which are like the quibbles of an old lackey or a wily minister.

I need you.

I need a man who can complain at the top of his voice, ringing the echoes of heaven where God deliberates with Satan to plot against a man.

Speak, lift up your voice. Speak loud. God can speak much louder than you – he has the thunder. But thunder is an answer . . . more magnificent than the saws and truisms on the justice of providence invented by human wisdom and hawked around by gossiping old women and eunuchs. . . .
(Kierkegaard, *La Répétition*, pp. 142–4)

God listens to Job.

At the end of the argument he condemns the orthodox. 'You have not spoken of me what is right, as my servant Job has.' The comforters are condemned to offer a sacrifice, and God adds: 'My servant Job shall pray for you' (Job 42.7–8).

So the world of the downtrodden redeems the world of the learned.

'Father, forgive them; for they know not what they do.'

'To my last breath I shall refuse to love this creation in which children are tortured.'[1]

That remark sums up very well all Albert Camus's generosity and the courage in pessimism which he sometimes relied on in the face of absurdity, suffering, and death.

The priest and the doctor who clash in *La Peste* are both figures of great nobility. I have to admit that, while Dr Rieux makes me proud to be a man, Father Paneloux's difficulty in justifying his faith in the face of the immensity of suffering scarcely satisfies me. I am not a priest of the religion in which faith exempts one from understanding.

A note of Camus's, taken from his *Notebooks*, throws a little light on the argument:

What distinguishes the religions of the priest and the doctor is that the priest thinks he possesses all science while the true doctor knows that he knows nothing. . . .[2]

I note that, in his comparison, Camus begins with 'the priest', but when he comes to the doctor he is clearly only interested in the 'true' doctor. . . . Why didn't he talk about the 'true' priest? And again, let's be fair. Depending on the priest or the doctor one has met, one could easily reverse the formula. Haven't we all known a doctor who has harmed us because he 'thought he possessed all science', and met 'a true priest' who could listen and keep quiet?

In the world there is the enormous problem of evil. Faith can no more avoid it or reduce it than revolt can. It is the wall. It blocks all reflection. The only escape is to take up the burden: only freedom can make any progress here. Only freedom has the power to assert its superiority over the evil which weighs it down. And it is well known that wherever a bit more freedom springs up in the world, love can shoot out and dissolve the evil.

Intelligence, love, and freedom are all faithful allies: creative power calls them together to push back evil.

In the same way the conductor of an orchestra, if he has any talent, knows his prestige: each of his movements and glances transmits to the orchestra and to the crowd a fluidity greater than himself. And there is music.

But it takes only a single hesitation, a single slip, his hand or his eyes moving slightly too late, to bring disaster. Then the orchestra is shamed and the public is disgusted. So who will they blame if the drums and cymbals have drowned the flute and the oboes?

I believe that in the admirable symphony of the world, that vast chorale of shadows and lights, it is human freedom that is on the rostrum.

We are at the mercy of clumsy freedoms.

In *La Peste*, it is the appalling sight of a child dying that makes Camus's hero exclaim, 'To my last breath I shall refuse to love this creation in which children are tortured.' Nothing is more horrible, nothing is more absurd or more unjust, than an innocent child suffering and dying without knowing what he is paying for. And I can understand that that makes people revolt against God. But creation is not implicated, much less God. I appeal to the human community, to society (I appeal to freedom), which make such misfortunes possible.

I remember a young man of eighteen, a prisoner at Fresnes, whom I met in those sinister surroundings of bars and bolts. He threw himself on me, wild-eyed and sobbing. 'Father, there's a curse on me. Bless me. Do something! My father was in prison, my mother was in prison, and now it's my turn. The mark of evil is on me. I'm a thief because my father was a thief. My life's a mess. There's a curse on me.'

Is it God we should hate? Is it creation we should accuse? Or, more tragically perhaps, isn't it our human community which in the end must admit and recognize in such cases of distress the mistakes of freedoms not quite achieved?

After all, we know very well that our society today has to take decisions of a gravity we cannnot measure. Will we be justified in accusing God and creation if, in a few decades, the pollution of nature sends us drifting towards other disasters? Will we be justified in accusing God and creation if the choices of today, dominated by profit, to sell arms, to sell death, turn against us?

The nuclear power stations we are promised may send us into ecstasies, but it doesn't need much knowledge to realize the enormous risks represented by the radioactive waste which will take centuries to decay and which must be kept somewhere. In these conditions who can guarantee today the security of man in terms of millennia? And will it be God and creation that we will have to accuse if, in two or three centuries, innocent children die as a result of our choices today?

We have here a measure, judged by our failures and our successes, by all the possibilities offered to us – the life or death of man – of the enormous power entrusted to us.

But will the men and women of our time finally realize that this is where political commitment is decided, on this level of greatness at which the voter, in the solitude of the voting booth, chooses something very different from his partisan passion, his personal profit, his dearest ideology?

He chooses man.

In the voting booth it is my freedom which is on trial, before history. It is not an isolated gesture for fragmentary interests. It is a creative act. I believe that at that solemn moment at which a free man, really free, casts his vote, he can recover instantly the whole of his dimension before God, who confers on him, there more than anywhere else, the responsibility of creating.

Hitler was a monster. Who put him into power? And in the face of that formidable revulsion in which the world vomited out its fury and hate in fire and blood, in the face of that insane war in which tens of millions of innocent men, women, and children met an absurd death, should we accuse God? Reject creation?

So Paul in his letter to the Romans:

> For the creation waits with eager longing for the revealing of the sons of God; for the creation was subjected to futility, not of its own will but by the will of him who subjected it [man] in hope; because the creation itself will be set free from its bondage to decay and obtain the glorious liberty of the children of God. We know that the whole creation has been groaning in travail together until now. (Rom. 8.19–22)

So we are brought back to the first chapters of this book. Adam and Eve in front of the tree of knowledge. Man facing his destiny. And God's anxious voice in the lost paradise, in the world which our choices have made dangerous: 'Adam, where are you?'

We have to choose. Life or death.

But let's come back to the Book of Job.

When we reread it, we must start from these weighty questions. Even when it appeared, centuries before Christ, it must have been a sensation. At that time any illness, any sort of misfortune, was a sign of disgrace. They were treated as punishment for sin, as the direct reply of God, who thus chastised those who did not keep his law.

Job rises against this incorrect theology.

> Far from ever admitting you to be in the right:
> I will maintain my innocence to my dying day.
> I take my stand on my integrity, I will not stir:
> my conscience gives me no cause to blush for my life.
> (Job 27.5–6, JB)

> If only I knew how to reach him [God],
> or how to travel to his dwelling!
> I should set out my case to him. . . .
> Would he use all his strength in this debate with me?
> No, he would have to give me a hearing.
> He would see he was contending with an honest man,
> and I should surely win my case.
> (Job 23.3–4, 6–7, JB)

This I know: that my Avenger lives,
    and he, the Last, will take his stand on earth.
After my awaking, he will set me close to him,
    and from my flesh I shall look on God.
    (Job 19.25–6, JB)

Cover not my blood, O earth,
    afford my cry no place to rest.   (Job 16.18, JB)

Silence! Now I will do the talking,
    whatever may befall me.
I put my flesh between my teeth,
    I take my life in my hands.
Let him kill me if he will; I have no other hope
    than to justify my conduct in his eyes.
This very boldness gives promise of my release. . . .
    (Job 13.13–16, JB)

Who can get me a hearing from God?
    I have had my say, from A to Z; now let Shaddai
      answer me.

I will give him an account of every step of my life,
    and go as boldly as a prince to meet him.
    (Job 31.35, 37, JB)

The great poet who wrote the Book of Job belongs to the race of the mystics. He met God on the other side of all the laws, all the theologies, all the traditions of his time.

I knew you then only by hearsay;
    but now I have seen you with my own eyes.

He knows that his God is the God of free men, He knows that faithfulness often means challenging, and that it is man's greatness 'to go boldly as a prince' to meet his God.

The author of the book puts into the mouth of his hero all the curses of the oppressed just man, all man's confusion before the unfathomable problem of evil and innocent suffering.

He presents to us, and with what humour, the laughable solemnity of the casuists and theologians of his time, and the immensity of human stupidity over which they reign. (One thinks of Molière's doctors!)

But the point of the story is in its conclusion. The last chapters, indeed, are a poem of sumptuous grandeur, God's defence.

Brace yourself like a fighter;
  now it is my turn to ask questions and yours to inform
  me. . . .

God counter-attacks. He invites Job to the battle. Man and
his God, here they are again, both of them. Face to face, and
so magnificent! And here we see once more man's most splen-
did dimension, his noblest boast: he is 'relation' to God.

Job and Yahweh.

This is Adam, the 'earthling', the 'man of the soil' (*adamah*,
soil), but he has received the breath of God and knows it.

This is Abraham in ecstasy at the moment of the 'alliance'
before the brazier, the fire of God passing between the bleed-
ing portions of the sacrificed victims.

This is the strange duel between Jacob and God.

All the great heroes of the Bible, all the prophets, all the
great mystics of every age, show us the same boldness, the same
pride in the relation of man to God. It culminates in the 'Our
Father' left to us by Jesus as the prayer worthy of God and
worthy of man and his last look towards the Father which is
now our look too: 'Everything which is yours is mine. . . .
Father, I am coming to you.'

In the grand finale of the Book of Job God defends himself in
masterly fashion against all Job's attacks, against all our attacks.

To the problems – even the most heart-rending – which Job
hurls at him, God gives no answer. He is not a magic God.
Neither Zeus nor Jupiter.

God is a *grand seigneur*. He cannot be approached except in
the depth of the mystery in which man's intelligence and heart
can sink: as you let yourself be swallowed up by the sea when
you dive with a mask and discover, to your astonishment, a
new world, a silent dream world, here where neither the
storms nor the waves which rage on the surface can trouble the
sovereign calm of the blue-lit depths.

It is in this way, I think, that intelligence is called to grapple
with the mystery. For contemplation. For total freedom. This
is how God appears to Job at the end of the poem.

He unfolds before Job's eyes the immense spectacle of his
creation.

The creator God, the poet God, who established the earth
'when all the stars of the morning were singing with joy'.

At his call the sea 'leapt out of the womb', and he made mist its garments and 'black clouds its swaddling bands'.

It is God who sent 'the dawn to its post, telling it to grasp the earth by its edges'.

Here are 'the gates of Death', the porters of the land of shadow, the storehouses of the snow and the hail, the thunder and lightning, the rain and the hoar-frost. Here is the dance of the stars:

Can you fasten the harness of the Pleiades,
    or untie Orion's bands?
Can you guide the morning star season by season
    and show the Bear and its cubs which way to go?
    (Job 38.31-2, JB)

Here are all the beasts of the earth, the lioness crouching in her den, the young ravens crying out to God, 'the hinds in labour', and the horse 'quivering with impatience'; the wisdom of the ibis, the intelligence of the cock, and nobility of the eagle soaring above inaccessible rocks.

God even gives much space to the nightmare monsters which inhabit the great waters, Behemoth and Leviathan – probably the hippopotamus and the crocodile – which are symbols of all the forces of evil, but which God dominates.

This is God's reply to Job. To man's cries of revolt against the disorder of the world, against evil and suffering, he replies with the splendours of his creation.

Because he has given his creation to man. To man's freedom. 'Fill the earth and subdue it' (Gen. 1.28).

Yes, this is God's reassurance, and the revolt stops short. God doesn't 'explain' suffering; he comes to share it.

Console my people, console them. . . .
Speak to the heart of Jerusalem
and call to her
that her time of service is ended,
that her sin is atoned for. . . .
Go up on a high mountain,
joyful messenger to Zion.
Shout with a loud voice. . . .

Shout without fear,
Say . . ., 'Here is your God.'
Here is the Lord . . . coming with power.
  (Isa. 40.1–2, 9–10, JB)

This is God appearing to man in the Book of Isaiah.

And since Jesus we know that, while man may be unhappy in flesh and blood, God becomes flesh and blood.

Man is swallowed up in doubt and fear, but Jesus comes to cry out in doubt and fear on Golgotha. 'My God, my God, why have you deserted me?' (Matt. 27.46, JB).

And if someone has to die in violence, hatred, and contempt to free the world and reveal to it its destiny of light beyond the grave, God comes to die on the cross.

It is to this God that I have given my life, and I, in my turn, want to shout out one of the finest outbursts of the man Job:

This I know: that my Avenger lives. . . .
And from my flesh I shall look on God.
I put my flesh between my teeth,
I take my life in my hands.
This very boldness gives promise of my release. . . .

NOTES

1 Camus, *La Peste*, Pléiade edn, p. 1395.
2 Camus, *La Peste*, 'Notes et variantes', p. 1988.

Death and Resurrection

The dead sleep comfortably in this earth.
It warms them and dries up their mystery. . . .
They have melted into a thick absence.
The red clay has drunk the white substance
and the gift of life has passed into the flowers.
Where are their familiar phrases,
the personal style, the unique souls?
Maggots crawl where the tears formed.
(Valéry)

I hate death.

I have been criticized for uttering those words publicly.
They were shocking in the mouth of a Christian, I was told.
Still I insist that it is possible to believe passionately in one's
resurrection and to hate death. 'I may be a Christian, but I'm
still human.' When Tartuffe says this, he is being his least Tar-
tuffish. The mask has fallen.

It seems to me dishonest to talk about the resurrection in a
way that makes it look like an easy excuse for getting round
the reality of biological death. My faith in the resurrection
does not remove the tragic mystery of death. It is a way – in
my view the only real way – of accepting the absurdity of
death with the maximum of freedom. The implacable violence
of death makes my life a destiny.

The hope of the resurrection makes my life freedom.

My death is inside me, watching me. I catch it lying in wait
each time a danger, inside me or outside me, threatens me.
Each instinctive reflex movement which spontaneously protects
me against brutal peril shows me that my death was there.

And life – 'my' life – is also on the watch, in a permanent
state of mobilization. Right at the bottom of my consciousness,
my life is a watching-out for death. I want to continue.

The old man walks more slowly. Death is at the end of the
road.

The man in the condemned cell experiences the most appalling absurdity. In him, life, with all its thrusting, its energy,
its dreams, and that powerful movement towards becoming,
life, that creative ferment, is a pure lie. His living consciousness
is the certainty of death. A man in a red gown asked for the
death penalty for him. Ordinary people said yes. That's when
they kill him. He is killed before he dies.

In that moment when we snatch from a man the hope of
continuing to become, we turn a living being into a consciousness of death. In the terrible interval between his sentencing
and his execution, the condemned man knows that he has been
robbed of his soul.

He is death.

That is monstrous. That is hideous. More hideous than the
executioner's movement. It disgraces a system of justice.

All days move towards death; the last one arrives.
(Montaigne, *Essays*, I, xx)

I have often felt the certainty of my death as a sort of absurdity. What is love, if we have to die?

I revolt against it, and my revolt itself has no future. Death
exists.

I am not talking just about the brutal death which strikes
down a creature in full flight. Who does not know that icy
numbness, that confusion verging on madness, that frightening
silence, or that animal cry which brings us all down to the
level of fear and the absurd when death has passed by?

It came in without knocking, overturning all the settings
in which life was so pleasant. A beloved creature is dead. That
is the absurdity: the brutal breaking-off of a destiny, the annihilation of possibilities, the bitterness, the tearing of tenderness, the sudden ageing, the anguish and dizziness of continuing without them, now.

Even if I consider death natural, 'normal', something which
gently snuffs out the old man who reaches the end of his time;
even if, facing some sorts of disintegration of the human
person, I too recognize that 'it was better for him to go', there
remains in me a deep instinct which tells me that death is
illegitimate.

People die too soon.

The dying old man, withered and comatose, still clenches

his skinny hands on the sheet. His last moment is a moment of life which doesn't want to die, of life which is not made to die.

It's not difficult to talk wisely about death in general: it's always someone else's death. But the subject becomes more serious if it means discovering in myself the infallible signals telling me in my secret silence that already 'my normal death' has lifted its unmoving face towards me and has me in sight. I am marked: weariness, wear, a failing organism, a hesitating memory, inform me discreetly of the insidious approach of death, of 'my' death.

And the instinctive movement of the driver who eases off on the accelerator because he has seen an accident is more than an act of prudence. In the confusion of the blue flashers of the ambulances, and the police, a dead person is there, stretched out by the side of the road. I slow down: I have met 'my' death.

And yet death is commonplace; the newspaper, the radio, and the television tell me about it every day.

An aeroplane crashes: 120 dead. If it's at the other end of the world, it's a news item. If it's in France, it's already near me, and I am more involved.

If the list of victims includes the name of someone dear to me, the accident is no longer a news item. Death is no longer commonplace. It is tragic.

And if I find that the plane I decided at the last minute not to catch has blown up, the very gratuitousness of the reprieve, the sheer intensity of survival, and the happiness of those who surround me, give me the measure of the fragility of my treasures. 'I would have died.' How bright the sun is then! And how good it is to feel quietly the harmony of my body, all the throbbings and quiverings of life. I didn't catch the plane. I didn't catch death.

Death is commonplace.
Death is tragic.
Death is ordinary.
Death is unique.
Death is a familiar habit.
Death is a tragic scandal.
Death is accepted by all.
Death is rejected by every fibre of every creature.

Death is here.
Death is fundamentally elsewhere.
Death is impossible.
Death is necessary.
Death is a certainty.
Death is uncertain.

That must be meaninglessness.

The last moment of consciousness is still a moment of life. To know that one is dying is to be still alive.

Death is the absolute extinction of 'biological becoming'. The elusive moment.

I remember a minor operation for which I was put to sleep with a mask. Even the preparations had quite interested me, because my wrists, ankles, and knees had been firmly fastened with straps. 'It's because of the reactions under the anaesthetic,' the nurse told me.

So they put me to sleep, and I must say that I experienced a few moments of real panic. The strange resonance of my own breathing inside the mask, the mysterious gas which invaded my lungs, the gradual heaviness which, little by little, robbed me of myself, all that suddenly released in me an instinctive violence which must have justified the straps. But I was no longer aware of my body's revolts. I only knew that I was sinking away. The surgeon's voice in my ear, at first distinct, gradually became like a liquid gurgle and faded into a fleecy mist, into the terrible silence, the black silence in which I was the only one, absolutely the only one, to know that I was still conscious. There was a moment when I tipped into nothingness . . . but that I didn't 'know'. Thank God, when I woke up – a few minutes later – life was good.

I remember trying to analyse each moment of that nightmare – it was so much like death – but I could only recall the writhing of all the instincts struggling for life, the terror of consciousness as it faded, irrevocably. But the moment of nothingness cannot be recaptured.

Is my death mine?

Any consideration of the resurrection which tried to elude these moments of panic seems to me an imposture.

On this point the Bible is honest and gives us the Book of

Ecclesiastes. A book with no illusions, in which black humour strips away any illusion about the destiny of man, life, suffering, freedom, pleasure, work, death: 'All is vanity.'

> . . . rather than the living who still have lives to live, I salute the dead who have already met death; happier than both of these is he who is yet unborn and has not seen the evil things that are done under the sun.   (Eccles 4.2–3, JB)

> Naked from his mother's womb he [the rich man] came, as naked as he came he will depart again; nothing to take with him after all his efforts. This is a grievous wrong, that as he came, so must he go; what profit can he show after toiling to earn the wind, as he spends the rest of his days in darkness, grief, worry, sickness and resentment?   (Eccles. 5.14–16, JB)

Here, death is no longer, as in so many books of the Bible, retribution for sin. It is part of the system, a presumably absurd system, which reduces a man's fate to that of a beast.

> Indeed, the fate of man and beast is identical; one dies, the other too, and both have the selfsame breath; man has no advantage over the beast, for all is vanity. Both go to the same place; both originate from the dust and to the dust both return. Who knows if the spirit of man mounts upward or if the spirit of the beast goes down to the earth?   (Eccles. 3.19–21, JB)

So spoke Qoheleth, the author of Ecclesiastes. In the name of lucidity, his little book rejects the over-simple explanations of the theologians of his time about the meaning of life and death. At that time there was still no knowledge at all of the resurrection.

For Qoheleth, God exists, and what he does 'he does consistently'. Qoheleth leaves everything to him and accepts all the futility of the human condition. He writes his thought without illusion, and even with deep bitterness.

> . . . my son, be warned that writing books involves endless hard work, and that much study wearies the body.   (Eccles. 12.12, JB)

Nevertheless, through these disillusioned pages there runs a profound intuition which challenges faith and marks an important stage in biblical thought's long and faltering journey in search of God.

People die too soon.

The number of years makes no difference. Let us make no mistake: neither age nor youth can be measured in terms of time. I know old people whose faces glow with light and freshness. They are liberated, as though death had nothing more to take from them. Even their memories are purified, and the failings of their frail bodies can no longer affect the bloom of youth in their eyes and their smiles.

And one also meets senile young people.

It is true that at the age of fifty the extent of my past makes me more hesitant about my future. I don't know what's left in my account. One day I shall make a plan which will be an unmet cheque.

I am programmed. To a great extent and in many respects, yes, I am programmed. That's a dangerous word, which conjures up determinism and fatalism, though I have no intention of minimizing the enormous power of freedom, which gives meaning to my life. I simply mean that arrangement of possibilities and potentialities summoned to develop in time, to develop within certain limits.

A creature constructs itself out of a genetic inheritance, a given quantity of information – given but unknown.

I only know that my stock of information is running down, towards death. That is the sense in which I speak of a programme, and that is perhaps the source of the revolt.

I live to die.

Life, which is felt as the absolute contradiction of death, life is 'for death'.

I know very well that it is possible to conquer anguish and 'find' oneself, at that culminating point of freedom at which it accepts death.

And it is possible to reach that magnificent triumph of serenity over all the panics which are the unnerving retinue of death.

That is perhaps man's noblest attitude towards his death. That is freedom. The hero and the saint are greater than the death which nevertheless destroys them.

And even if some people have chosen to demand their own

deaths, if they have fixed the day and the hour when they will bring about their deaths, that is only a pseudo-freedom.

Who can decide that he has no more possibilities?

We are programmed. The 'programme' is the substratum of the person. But I do not know my programme. I know nothing of that inheritance of information, of potentialities, which can only be realized in time. And the pride which wants to escape the humiliation of decaying senility and assigns itself a time to die, is resigning itself to the worst humiliation of freedom, flight. It is taking the wild risk of blocking the programme and, whatever happens, mutilating creation.

And then, man is communal. His illness, his ageing, his death, are not solitary. Quite the reverse; they provoke the whole human community to react and fight, because it sees its destiny as depending on my own becoming.

One can imagine the collective resignations into which we would all drift together as a result of some law justifying unconditional 'euthanasia'.

But accepting death, welcoming it, or demanding it is taking a position in relation to the problem. It is not solving it.

Death is a mystery.

Is death destiny?

I am there – 'thrown there' – sentenced to freedom – sentenced to loneliness: we die alone.

So, to the attack: loneliness must be broken. Connection with others is already the anti-death. The sexual connection is perhaps the most extraordinary negation of death. To blow loneliness apart. To bind my destiny to that of the other, to 'superexist'. To make the other exist outside himself or herself. To exist outside myself through the other. The power of sex climbs back up the slope. To have a child is to snatch possibilities from non-being and invent new 'programmes'.

This is the orchestration of life and the overwhelming beauty of the couple. The couple affirms the eternity of life by celebrating tenderness in the flesh.

I have just betrayed myself; I said 'eternity of life'. It's true; I don't believe in nothingness. Nothingness is an illusion. It is, so they say, 'non-being'. But to talk about it is already to make it exist as a 'something'. I do not believe in the existence of the non-existent, in the 'being' of non-being, even if it is reduced to the very volatile form of a concept.

I don't yet want to bring in my faith. I'm deliberately trying to go to the limit of this feeling that my death is absurd.

My faith in the resurrection doesn't solve the problem; it shatters it. All that's left is biological death – a small problem if I continue.

It seems to me, however, that the feeling 'death is absurd', shows me in turn a still deeper tension: 'I am, therefore I should continue.'

Being is becoming, that is, essentially, continuing. What has been, what is, cannot, by definition, subsequently tip into non-being. My body crumbles, but I continue.

So what is it in me that wants to continue in the face of the plain fact of death? At this point one could cite Spinoza or Bergson and console oneself with metaphysical arguments, but metaphysics too can be an alibi, an escape. I don't believe that death can be reduced simply to the metaphysical problem it poses.

I remember a conversation about death with an unbeliever, in which both of us tried to be clear. I remember a secret he told me. He and his wife had promised each other that they would not be present at the other's last moment, but would withdraw, whatever the cost, so that the memory preserved of the beloved creature would be one of life, the light in the eyes, the wonderful smile. 'Life! Life is the only thing that counts!' Even if this decision looks like an irrevocable profession of un-belief, nevertheless at the deep level of this conversation (in which my friend and I had reached an amazing intimacy: the sort in which silences and looks say more than words), this admission struck a chord in me among certainties even more powerful than that secret, stubborn will to continue.

I was reminded at this point of what I have always known: it is love that wants to live. I know that it is possible not to share this point of view. It is possible, I am told, to love deeply even within the limits of a transitory life, to accept that the adored face which is 'the joy of my heart, the joy of my eyes', as the Bible says, is only the mask for a death's-head, destined to end in a hole in the earth.

'Man knows that he dies,' said Malraux. That is his tragic superiority over the animals.

But I find that the more culture matures and the more the

power to love becomes personalized and refined, death, which primitive peoples anticipate and accept with amazing serenity, is for us absurdity, the great fear.

It is love which wants to continue – which ought to continue. That is perhaps the most important meaning of the story I mentioned just now. The person who wants the only memory he has of the person he loves to be that of his or her living face is also rejecting the death of his love.

I remember that hearing this secret shook me, because it suddenly activated in me all the harmonics of my faith, and in the solemn silence which united us I heard Jesus's promises in the Gospel of John. They are all 'promises of life'.

I am the LIVING bread.
Anyone who eats this bread will LIVE for ever.
This bread which I shall give is my flesh for the LIFE of the world.
Anyone who eats my flesh and drinks my blood has eternal LIFE.
Anyone who believes in me will have eternal LIFE.
I am the way, the truth, and the LIFE.
Whoever follows me will have the light of LIFE.
Truly, truly, I say to you, the hour is coming, and has already come, when even the dead will hear the voice of the Son of God, and those who hear it shall LIVE for ever.

It is to these texts that I am indebted for being able to master what I previously called the absurdity of death.

But nothing is changed. I still experience the passage of death with an extreme violence; and the threat of death which constantly hovers round me, the insidious penetration of death into my life, come up in me against an invincible will to endure. This is an argument which perhaps derives from instinct, but it is one which no judgement will ever settle: the certainty of death against the intuition of continuance.

This is the point where I could perhaps insert my faith in the resurrection and offer it as a support to this powerful appeal to continue.

Perhaps, but no.

My faith in the resurrection doesn't come from my instincts. It isn't biological. It is rooted in the contemplation of the God of whom I believe passionately that he is the human dimension.

My faith in the resurrection doesn't depend on reasoning, or on a form of education, or on a theological culture.

I started to believe that I will rise again, like any good Christian, because that is what we were taught from our earliest years. But I challenge the good Christian to face the mystery of his own death to its furthest limits and be reassured by what he has been taught about the resurrection.

In any case, my faith in the resurrection doesn't reassure me. It frees me, and that is quite different. It is in my faith that I make my death my own.

My death is no longer destiny. It is liberty.

Everything I said at the beginning of this chapter stands; it was a single, frail man arguing with himself in the face of an absurd destiny.

My faith in the resurrection accepts humbly all the distress of death. It does not originate from me. It does not originate in me.

It is the fruit of an infinite tenderness in which the relation of man to God which has never ceased to obsess me throughout this book, reaches its culminating point: our God is the God of the living.

He is living.

He is life.

The seed of divinity has been planted in me, and my passion for life, so pure and so tortured, surrounded by anxieties and with the obsession of death constantly gnawing at it, a great soaring wave in which tenderness and joy are nevertheless feasting and dancing, wild flames of my desires, this passion of mine for life suddenly becomes intoxicated with infinity because I have raised my eyes and met the transfigured face of Jesus risen.

The intimacy of man with God is celebrated on Easter Day.

I want to wrap myself in the admirable prologue of John's Gospel, and let myself be swept up, drunk with freedom, into that blast of the divine into the human.

. . . the Word was God.
. . . the Word became flesh.
[He] is in the bosom of the Father.   (John 1.1, 14, 18)

These are the three powerful pegs by which the destiny of man rises again.

They recur in Paul's letter to the Philippians:

His state was divine . . .
but [he] emptied himself . . .
and became as men are.   (Phil. 2.6–7, JB)

But God . . . gave him the name
which is above all other names.   (Phil. 2.9, JB)

God plunges into man, and man rises powerfully in God; it is an invincible current, a groundswell which draws man up in the wake of the risen Jesus towards his eternal destiny, where it breaks in fullness.

'Death, where is your victory?' exclaims the apostle Paul.

Bodies may teem with worms in the empty silence of the graves: I am alive!

And the 'eternal laugh' which Valéry talked about is not his 'empty skull'. It is the drunkenness of fullness, of the totality of being; it is love and freedom, constantly insatiable and constantly sated, and intelligence like a great furnace of light, and joy rising and falling like the swell of the great oceans.

These are the units in which man and his destiny should be measured. He was created to this scale, God's scale, of the vastness of love.

The fleshly earth is therefore not the 'vale of tears' in which we stagger about while waiting for a better life.

Eternity is not a beautiful dream to help us bear a life which is a mockery in a failed world, to escape the problem of death by taking refuge in another place.

No, the life we lead on earth with its limits, its dreams, its battles, its pains, and its joys, now takes on all its meaning, because eternity is here, now.

It is more than a promise.

It is a reality in my life.

It is the success of my life.

No, I don't live in order to die. On the dust of the earth I walk with eternal steps, and, even today, my life is the happiness of existing in this light. And the humblest joys and the most oppressive restrictions, in which, as time goes by, the power to love develops, freedom is fashioned and intelligence grows, everything derives its meaning from this movement towards surplus being in its fullness.

Suffering, that terrible price of freedom, so often a source of despair, also finds its meaning and can take root in hope.

Death and its vile retinue, death itself, is conquered. It is the necessary crossing in which my hope is fulfilled.

From now on I live my death rather than dying to life.

Now I have come to the other extreme from the first pages of this chapter, to find that death has another face, turned towards the light.

It is like the strange figure at the doorway of the Virgin at Notre-Dame in Paris, a man with two faces. One, turned towards the light and warmth of summer, glows with youth; the other, bent towards the darkness and cold of winter, is an old man's face. It is perhaps the sublimation of the old myth of Janus, who had the power to bring together before his eyes the past and the future. I would like to see in it the meaning of death and the enormous leap from fleshly age into eternal youth.

Death and resurrection.

The moment of my death is the moment of my resurrection.

I know that this chapter is paradoxical in going deliberately from death as absurdity to death as liberation. But this passage is the pivot of Christian faith. Easter, the Passover – the word means passing over.

There is no transition.

There is no argument.

There is not even continuity.

Reasoning stops.

It is a leap, not a leap into the absurd but a dive into mystery.

Plato and Descartes trapped the western mind in a logical system from which it can no longer escape, and Cartesian criteria have become infallible and implacable laws which can scarcely comprehend intelligence's plunge into mystery.

The God of Jesus Christ is not the God of the philosophers.

We accept that poets and artists have the power to make good the failings of intelligence, and yet they soar away from the rigid rigours of reasoning. But we distrust mystics, although contemplation and transcendence are perhaps the most admirable forms of knowledge because it is there above all that intelligence recognizes itself to be the fullness of love and sovereign freedom.

The revelation of a God who gives himself is not a proof; it is testimony.

I believe in love.

Death is conquered.

Love and death, two solemn words which in conjunction are for me the essence of the supreme confrontation.

Love wins.

Jesus Christ is risen.

One might have thought that it was all over.

One might have thought that it would all stop there, in the icy silence of the three crosses erected under a louring sky.

The gospel tells us the story of the implacable destiny of Jesus of Nazareth and his three years' public life.

It was a time for boldness. It was a time of battles.

And a time of contempt and a time of fear.

Jesus of Nazareth.

He had denounced pride and lying and hatred and injustice, and human inertia, with an extraordinary passion.

He had mastered anguish.

He had gone beyond suffering.

He had faced death.

And then in a few hours the whole business was settled.

The astonishing adventure ended on the cross, in tears and blood, in loneliness and mocking laughter.

It is all over.

His best friends, pursued by fear, scattered.

The gospel describes the conversation of two of them in those days. They are on the road and walking towards the village of Emmaus.

They are already talking about Jesus in the past tense: 'He was a great prophet.' 'We hoped he would deliver Israel.'

It was over.

The cross set the seal on the failure.

And yet on the joyful Easter morning the news was on all lips: 'He is alive.'

Three days after all the noise on Golgotha.

Three days after the loud cry from the cross, 'My God, my God, why have you forsaken me?'

Three days after the apparent failure comes the triumphal return: he is alive.

Today Pilate, Caiaphas, and all the others are no more than miserable nonentities, the playthings of the history they thought they controlled.

From now on all our hopes are alive with his risen life.

Jesus Christ, son of man and Son of God, offers us his victory over death, and his resurrection is a hymn to life.

But all this is addressed to faith.

To faith, because if one studies carefully the texts which reveal the fact of the resurrection of Jesus, if one puts them together and corrects each by the others, to find the best arrangement and combination, one soon finds that the texts offer little scope for scientific methods of investigation and that they fail to satisfy the criteria of historians.

The reason is that the gospels are not biographies of Jesus, and all the testimonies they give us of his birth, life, death, and resurrection are intended first and foremost to be a support for a message which itself depends entirely on faith.

That is why there is little use in continuing to ask questions about the empty tomb: an angel is there on that Easter morning – an angel, that is, a messenger from God (that is, the word of God) – to give us the meaning of the empty tomb and to shatter, perhaps to disappoint, the rigour of our investigations, and to bring us face to face with the extraordinary truth to which alone faith can cling:

He is risen.
He is not here.

Here intelligence has to make an unusual sacrifice if it ventures into the gospel texts. It has to discover the writer's intention and the source from which he drew his inspiration. It has to recreate the very particular sensibility and receptivity of each of the communities for which each gospel was written in the first place.

The gospels belong to a period when the sense of history had none of the scientific rigour with which we are familiar today. We are dealing with a supremely biblical culture and view of man in which the influence of Plato is still slight, in which

Descartes does not exist to dissect the human person into a body of darkness which is only the prison of the soul of light.

In other words, the very idea of resurrection, right from its origin, has gone completely beyond the norms and laws of our western imagination, fed as it has been by exact sciences, and fashioned by philosophers and scholars.

And this is perhaps the place to reaffirm that while intelligence must never give up, while its role is to pursue its investigation in an attempt to resolve the 'problems' presented by the texts, while it is true that faith's demand that we believe can never dispense us from understanding, the fact remains that though intelligence may try to solve the problems, it does not exhaust the mystery – for the mystery is God's revelation to man and envelops and engulfs us completely.

The problem of the empty tomb presents us with the inexhaustible mystery of Jesus risen.

The very heart of the matter is faith, entering clearsightedly into the faith of the first Christian communities, which also relied on the faith of the witnesses: 'He is risen. He is no longer here.'

My whole faith is there, summed up completely in those few words.

The gospels prove nothing.

They proclaim the truth which the first witnesses lived, beginning on Easter morning.

You who were in despair because your life hadn't fulfilled its promises, rejoice, for now everything is possible.

You who weep for dear ones who are dead, dry your tears; we have astounding news – they are alive.

You who reject all hope because you are left alone with the shreds of a great love in your hands, your torn love, your impossible love: lift up your head. Look. Jesus is the tenderness of God, and with him any love is now stronger than death.

And you who have given up, who have stopped fighting, defeated by your sin, yes, you especially, stop despising yourself. 'Get up and walk.' Jesus Christ is alive, and whatever happens, your destiny is light.

We know now that the cross, and suffering, are not failure.

They are the surest marker on our road, the guarantee to ensure that every human life, every love, will surge again

beyond the graves and burst in that great explosion of life,
seething and abundant, a living sheaf of light, love, and joy
which will flow down on us that Easter morning, to make the
earth sing and celebrate life.

I am the resurrection and the life, says Jesus. He who believes in me, though he die, yet shall he live.

And I believe, yes, I believe, that one day, your day,
my God, I shall advance towards you,
With my faltering steps,
With my tears in my hands,
And this marvellous heart which you have given us,
This heart which is too big for us because it was made for you.

One day I shall come, and you will read in my face
All the distress, all the struggles, all the failures of the roads to
   freedom,
And you will see all my sin.
But I know, O my God, that sin is not serious when one is
   before you.
It is before men that one is humiliated,
But before you it is wonderful to be so poor,
Because one is so greatly loved!

One day, O my God, I shall come towards you
And in the fearful explosion of my resurrection
I shall know at last
That you are tenderness,
That you are also my freedom.

I shall come towards you, O my God, and you will show me
   your face.
I shall come to you with my wildest dream,
to bring you the world in my arms.

I shall come towards you and cry to you at the top of my voice
The whole truth of life on earth.
I shall cry my cry to you which comes from the beginning of
   time:
'Father, I have tried to be a man, and I am your child.'

Avigny; July, August, September 1974

Postscript
IN THE FORM OF A DIALOGUE BETWEEN
FRANCIS JEANSON AND THE AUTHOR

JACQUES LECLERCQ

I wrote this book above all to try to say that there is a point after which it becomes possible to be truthful together. It goes back to that meeting between my faith and your unbelief – and that is far beyond a simple intellectual encounter, as regards the reasons each of us may have for risking dialogue, the recognition of man by man.

FRANCIS JEANSON

And love, of course! All the same, you talk about love very well, because, on certain occasions, you've paid the price which allowed you to live it. But today I don't want to worry about us, about our choices and our privileges. Our two groups have already spent a lot of time trying to betray – in the best sense of the word – our respective causes, the atheists trying to rescue politics from its ideologists, the Christians trying to free the Spirit from his theologians.

But the fact is that of these two urgent tasks, we more or less chose to give priority to the second, the cleaning-up and purifying of the very idea of transcendence. Which means that we started dealing with God before worrying about men. I'm sure there were quite good reasons for doing that, but it did take us a long time to concern ourselves with men.

To say that God is love and that he became man doesn't allow us to conclude that man is love. It's high time to start thinking about everything in each of us which prevents us from expressing ourselves truthfully, loving and making ourselves lovable. We all, in different degrees, experience enormous difficulties in meeting our fellow human beings, in accepting their difference, in sharing with them the risks of a real meeting. We are all more or less fakes, forgeries, counterfeit, so much so that we can no longer trust what others say to us or what we say to them – let alone what we say to ourselves.

So, together, we staked everything on love, and your book is here as evidence, to assert to the death – and to the life! – that thirst for love which in our eyes is the only source of all human commitment. But the truthfulness of our ordinary undertakings also depends on the resources we allow ourselves to carry them out with. It is at this point, I think, that we must agree to accept our simple humanity, not just the finitude of our condition and its absolutely relational status, but also the enormous complexity of structures of all sorts, economic, social, and cultural, which we are condemned to interiorize in the very moment when they impose themselves on us in their most objective and most external forms.

This means that we always have to ask ourselves where we've got to, where I am, where you are, where he is, and what interference or noise threatens to disturb our so-called meetings. I have always had certain prejudices about the so-called 'human sciences' and those who claim to use them to define man while despising individual men. Nevertheless, in a book by Edgar Morin there is a short sentence which comes back to me from time to time, like certain poems or certain songs which I have been very fond of, '. . . perhaps, if we re-examine science by means of love, and love by means of science, we may try to see dimly how love might take its direction from love.'

There, that says it all, the finality, the profound resource, and even the means which we can and should employ. On this last point, the human sciences offer us, in our own case – both as individuals and as members of one or other collectivity – a multiplicity of illuminations which we need desperately if we are to avoid confusing our illusions with our moments of awareness, our alienations with our choices.

Your book talks about love. It takes a stand on the essential, it names the game, it tells the truth we want. But how are we to go about seeing that this truth becomes true? That it can be lived by any men and any women, by those who give the appearance of being normal and by those who are declared abnormal?

Are we normal, you and I? We conform to the norms, of course, since this society has not yet excluded us, but you know very well that this love your book talks about is pure folly in the eyes of our philosophers. It is at this point that we need extreme vigilance. The important people are not you or I, but all those we claim to be talking to; and we have no right to appeal to their deepest need without asking ourselves about the very context in which they will try to satisfy it.

What is human love apart from our individual adventures? It is this spiritual current which circulates (and never circulates enough) among men and which more or less allows them to want to be human; it is an accident, a gift, a grace – and often a quasi-absence. The whole problem is there: how can we encourage this circulation, increase its chances, given the disturbing opacity which each of us already presents to himself?

The men of today, we see it at every moment, are in total disarray. They have lost all the points of reference which their predecessors could rely on, but they are still perfectly capable of feeling frustrated in the deepest part of themselves, as though they had lost a dimension which in some way seems to them essential. And constantly, on all sides, men and women are calling for help, proclaiming their loneliness, demanding love. And we who talk about love, are we sure of always hearing them? And when we do hear them, well, what answers have we got to give them?

There is this infernal distance and our pretension of reducing it by some word of love, a gesture of brotherhood, a sign of tenderness. But only too often we fail – and it is important that we try to find out why.

I'm not going to push this idea very far, I still don't know enough about it; all the same, I want to say that one of the most terrible distances which can come to exist between men seems to me to result from knowledge – and only knowledge can enable us to overcome it. In one way, knowledge oppresses and alienates all of us: in each of us it is the negation of love, either because it gives us a means of dominating others or because it persuades us to let ourselves be dominated by them. There are those who know and there are the others: real power plays on this difference, which is much more insidious and much more difficult to fight than material domination. I think I know, and that stops me listening to the other person; or the other person thinks that I know and doesn't even imagine that he can talk to me about himself.

But our only weapon against this mystifying and mystified knowledge is a real effort to know. Recognizing another person means first of all taking the trouble to get to know his situation and appreciate its constraints. Here the human sciences have a role to play which seems to me crucial, and I do not believe that we can be satisfied with contrasting it with prophecy or charisms of whatever sort. Knowledge without faith is scientism and credulity. Faith without science is the hell of good intentions. Let us therefore together, prophets, philosophers, and researchers, give ourselves all the resources possible to create a social praxis which will be constantly kept fresh by a requirement of love.

JACQUES LECLERCQ
There's no need to stop. . . . We've already come a good way together, and now we're about to continue, this time towards new horizons.